India-Russia Strategic Partnership

Published in association with

Indian Council of World Affairs (ICWA), New Delhi

India-Russia Strategic Partnership

Challenges and Prospects

Edited by

NIVEDITA DAS KUNDU

ACADEMIC FOUNDATION

NEW DELHI

First published in 2010
by

ACADEMIC FOUNDATION
4772-73 / 23 Bharat Ram Road, (23 Ansari Road),
Darya Ganj, New Delhi - 110 002 (India).
Phones : 23245001 / 02 / 03 / 04.
Fax : +91-11-23245005.
E-mail : books@academicfoundation.com
www. academicfoundation.com

in association with
Indian Council of World Affairs (ICWA), New Delhi.

Cataloging in Publication Data--DK
Courtesy: D.K. Agencies (P) Ltd. <docinfo@dkagencies.com>
India-Russia strategic partnership : challenges and prospects / edited by Nivedita Das Kundu.
p. cm.
ISBN 13: 9788171888276
ISBN 10: 8171888275

1. India--Foreign relations--Russia (Federation)--Congresses. 2. Russia (Federation)--Foreign relations--India--Congresses. I. Kundu, Nivedita Das.

DDC 327.54047 22

Typeset by Italics India, New Delhi.
Printed and bound in India.

Contents

List of Tables and Figures 7
About the Editor/Contributors 9
Preface
SUDHIR T. DEVARE 13
Introduction
NIVEDITA DAS KUNDU 15

Section I
India-Russia Cooperation in Defence, Space and Energy Sector

1. India-Russia Defence Cooperation: Perspectives and Prospects
ARUN SAHGAL 25
2. Indo-Russian Space Cooperation
AJEY LELE 37
3. Hindrances in Indo-Russian Defence Cooperation
RAHUL K. BHONSLE 49
4. India-Russia Energy Cooperation
DEVIKA SHARMA 67
5. India-Russia Civil Nuclear Cooperation
G. BALACHANDRAN 85

Section II
India-Russian Economic Cooperation

6. Economic Subsystem of Russia-India Relations
LOUNEV SERGEY IVANOVICH 95

7. Indo-Russian Economic Linkages: A Critical Assessment
GULSHAN SACHDEVA 107

Section III

India and Russia in the Contemporary World

8. Russia and India in a Multidimensional World: An Experiment with Five Indices
IVAN TIMOFEEV 123

9. The National Interests of Russia in the Asia Pacific Region
DMITRI V. STRELTSOV 139

10. India-Russia Strategic Cooperation: Eye on the Future
NIVEDITA DAS KUNDU 151

Index *161*

List of Tables and Figures

Tables

7.1 India-USSR Trade Relations, 1960-61 to 1990-91 108
7.2 India-Russia Trade, 1993-94 to 2007-08 111
7.3A Commodity Composition of Indo-Russian Trade 112
7.3B Some Important Imports from Russia, 2006-07 and 2007-08 113
7.4 India-Russia Services Trade 114
7.5 Number of Agreements between Russia and India, 2000-2008 116
8.1 External and Internal Threats Rating: Selected Countries 129
8.2 Potential of International Influence Rating: Selected Countries 130
8.3 Quality of Life Rating: Selected Countries 131
8.4 Stateness Rating: Selected Countries 132
8.5 Institutional Basis of Democracy Rating: Selected Countries 133
8.6 Percentage of Countries' Explanation by the Principle Components: Selected Cases 134

Figures

4.1 India's Rising Demand for Energy 68
4.2A Coal Production and Import Dependency 69
4.2B Oil Production and Import Dependency 69
4.2C Natural Gas Production and Import Dependency 69

4.3 Russia's Consumption *versus* Reserves as Percentage of Total ... 71
4.4 India's Energy Imports from Russia ... 78
8.1 Countries in the Space of Principle Components 1 and 2 ... 135
8.2 Countries in the Space of Principle Components 1 and 4 ... 137

About the Editor and Contributors

Editor:

Nivedita Das Kundu (Ph.D.) is a Research Fellow, at the Indian Council of World Affairs (ICWA), New Delhi. Earlier she worked as an Associate Fellow with the Institute for Defence Studies and Analyses (IDSA) and as a Fellow with Department of Science & Technology (DST), New Delhi. She has also taught in the University of Helsinki (Finland) and in the University of Hannover (Germany). She has received her Doctorate from School of International Studies, Jawaharlal Nehru University, New Delhi. Her research interest includes: geopolitical issues, foreign policy and strategic dimensions of security with focus on Russia and the former Soviet States, including Afghanistan and multilateral organisations like SCO, BRIC, CSTO, NATO and EU. She has contributed widely on these research areas nationally and internationally. She has authored a book on *Russia and it's Near Abroad: Strategic Dynamics and Implications* and edited books on *Russia-India-China: Evolution of Geopolitical Strategic Trends.* She has published articles in various national and international journals, in edited books, in newspapers and in websites. She has also written policy briefs, issue briefs and occasional papers on her subject of expertise. She is also a recipient of number of prestigious national as well as international fellowships including DAAD (Germany), CIMO (EU), RAS (Russia), ICSSR (India) and Post-Doctoral Fellow Woodrow Wilson Center (US).

Contributors:

G. Balachandran is a Visiting Fellow at the Institute for Defence Studies and Analyses and Research Consultant at National Maritime Foundation. He is Ph.D. from the University of Wisonsin, Meadison, USA. He is a specialist on nuclear energy issues and expert on India's defence expenditure.

Rahul K. Bhonsle (Brig.), a military veteran with over three decades of active service, is now pursuing a second career in research at an independent agency, Sasia Security-Risks. His areas of interest include future warfare and human security. He is a regular contributor to leading mainstream and professional newspapers, websites and journals and edits a monthly, *South Asia Security Trends*. He is presently working on Net Assessment of the Indian Armed Forces.

Lounev Sergey Ivanovich (Ph.D.) is Professor at the Department of Oriental Studies and also at the Moscow State Institute of Foreign Relations. He has also worked as a Chief Research Fellow at the Institute of World Economics and International Relations, Russian Academy of Sciences. He has to his credit 192 published works, including 11 monographs.

Ajey Lele (Ph.D.) is an Indian Air Force officer (Wing Commander) and is working as a Research Fellow at the Institute for Defence Studies and Analyses (IDSA), New Delhi. He works on issues related to weapons of mass destruction (WMD) and strategic technologies with a major focus on space security. He is a postgraduate in Physics (Pune University) and has also done his M.Sc. and M.Phil. in Defence and Strategic Studies from Madras University. He has obtained his doctorate from Jawaharlal Nehru University (JNU), New Delhi. He has published articles in journals, websites and newspapers. He has authored two books titled: *Bio-Weapons: The Genie in the Bottle* and *Weather and Warfare*.

Gulshan Sachdeva (Ph.D.) is an Associate Professor at the Centre for European Studies, School of International Studies, Jawaharlal Nehru University, New Delhi. He is Visiting Professor at the University of Trento (Italy). His area of expertise is Russia and Central Asia (economic transformation), South Asia (Indian economy and foreign policy, SAARC), Europe, and Afghanistan (security, development, regional cooperation). Works mainly in the areas of macroeconomic policy reforms, regional economic integration, foreign policy and foreign economic relations, public sector reforms, privatisation and private sector development, economic policy formulation for conflict and post-conflict areas, civil service capacity development and training.

Arun Sahgal (Brig.) is Head, Center for Strategic Studies and Simulation, and Deputy Director Research, United Service Institution of India. In a career spanning over 36 years in the Indian army, he held number of important command, staff and instructional appointments. His most distinctive service assignment has been the Founder Director of the Office of Net Assessment, Integrated Defense Staff (Ministry of Defence)—an office, created to undertake long-term strategic assessments, to assist in national security planning and development of future military capabilities. His academic pursuits include Senior Fellow at the Institute for Defense Studies and Analyses and Distinguished Fellow, School of Geo-Politics, Manipal Academy of Higher Education. He recently completed a major Net Assessment study on India-China Military Balance 2025, for the Indian Joint Staff, and drafted India's National Security Strategy. He is independent consultant with Jane's Information Group and Booze Allen and Hamilton. He is a member of National Task Force on Net Assessment and Simulation under the National Security Council, Government of India.

Devika Sharma is an Associate Fellow at the Centre for Research on Energy Security at The Energy and Resources Institute (TERI), New Delhi. She submitted her doctoral thesis at Jawaharlal Nehru University, New Delhi from where she did her M.Phil. and M.A. in International Relations. Before joining TERI, she was with the Confederation of Indian Industry (CII) and the Observer Research Foundation, New Delhi.

Dmitri V. Streltsov (Ph.D.) is Professor Head of Eastern Studies Chair, Moscow State Institute for International Relations, Moscow. He is also a leading research fellow of the Center of Japanese Studies of the Institute of Oriental Studies, Russian Academy of Sciences. His research interest includes the internal political situation and foreign policy of Japan, Russo-Japanese relations and the problems of security in North-East Asia.

Ivan Timofeev (Ph.D.) is an Associate Professor and Chief Executive of the Centre for Analytical Monitoring, State Institute for International Relations, Moscow. He has 4 monographs and 30 research articles to his credit.

Preface

This book is the outcome of the conference titled "India-Russia Strategic Partnership: Challenges and Prospects", organised by the Indian Council of World Affairs (ICWA), New Delhi in collaboration with the Moscow State Institute of International Relations (MGIMO), Moscow, at Sapru House, New Delhi, on 28th-29th November 2008. In this book, the views expressed by both Indian and Russian academicians, policy makers and technical experts during the conference have been compiled. I hope that this publication proves useful to all those interested in strengthening the relations between India and Russia.

The strategic partnership between Russia and India has now endured well over 40 years. The bilateral ties between the two countries are based on continuity, trust and mutual understanding and are also driven by shared hopes to create a multipolar world. The developments in the post-Soviet years have added many new dimensions to the age-old bilateral relations. Today India-Russia relations have assumed a meaningful significance in the international context. Both countries are embarked on a path pursuing independent and flexible foreign policies in keeping with their respective national interests and aspirations to become important powers. In the conference, a serious effort was made to understand the realities of India-Russia relations in various fields such as defence, trade and economy, energy as well as space.

The book is divided into three sections. The first section deals with "India-Russia Cooperation in Defence and Energy Sector", the second section has been titled "India-Russia Economic Cooperation", and the third deals with "India and Russia in the Contemporary World". In the conference, mutual interest, challenges and opportunities for diversifying cooperation in various sectors were discussed. The conference reflected the changing dynamics of the situation in both the countries and their mutual needs and requirements to improve the bilateral relationship. It is expected that this book will fill the existing gap in the literature on this subject and provide a useful input to policy planners. The readers will find important information on both Russian and Indian perspectives and positions on various issues and concerns.

On behalf of ICWA, I express my sincere gratitude to MGIMO for enthusiastically collaborating with ICWA in organising this conference. Special thanks are due to Ambassador S.K. Lambah, Lt. Gen. (Retd.) Satish Nambiar and Ambassador V.B. Soni for providing their valuable time and inputs in chairing the sessions of the conference. I am also thankful to all the Indian and Russian contributors who have penned down their precious thoughts for this volume.

Sudhir T. Devare
Director General,
Indian Council of World Affairs,
New Delhi

Introduction

Nivedita Das Kundu

India-Russia bilateral relationship has been marked by close understanding and convergence of views on all major issues. Russia occupies a special place in India's foreign relations. Both the countries' geopolitical interests have always had much in common and both are optimistic about the future of strategic partnership. This partnership is genuinely strategic in nature, and is based on many years of evolution of fruitful relationship tested by time and dramatic events of historic dimensions. This multifaceted relationship has created a special atmosphere of trust and mutual understanding between the two countries. There is a clear reflection of the fact that India-Russia strategic cooperation will endure well into the future as there are obvious long-term interests between both the countries. The significance of this relationship is stressed by the fact that both countries are world powers and now also among the biggest economies.

The relations between India and Russia are quite unique. It is difficult to find other states that have so many common features that bring them together, like the closeness of the approaches to the global problems, similarities in its current policies and the geopolitical concerns. The ethno-religious composition of the two states, the similarity of civilisational features, the quantitative indicators (both states belong to the category of super large countries), etc., has strengthened their ties. Besides, Russians and Indians have friendly relations even at the grass-root level. Unfortunately, all this is often taken for granted. Both states tend to ignore the necessity to improve their image in the partner country.

Immediately after disintegration of the Soviet Union, there was a cardinal shift in Russian policy. The "Western school" approach, asserting that Russia's future should be intimately linked to Western civilisation, was rejected after experiencing severe humiliation and economic turmoil in the country. The ideas of "Oriental school" that claim that Russia should recognise and reconfirm its roots in the Asiatic cultural stock and abandon the search for illusory linkages with the West, were openly accepted by Russia inspite of its Euro-centric inclination. Russia's foreign policy emphasises the uniqueness of Russia's geopolitical, historic and cultural position as a "bridge" between Europe and Asia. However, over the years, Russia's foreign policy has gained multiple dimensions and Asia, especially India, as one of the most significant state ranks very high in its list of priorities.

This edited volume is the product of joint research essays by Russian and Indian experts. The emphasis of the three research essays contributed by the Russian participants is on the approaches of both countries for the development of the economic subsystem of the bilateral relations and the comparative analysis of the political system of Russia and India as well as convergence of ideas on the security of the Asia Pacific region.

The chapters written by prominent Indian experts cover the concrete dimensions of the bilateral relations: economic ties, cooperation in the energy sphere, defence and space cooperation. All authors are of the view that these links provide mutual benefits to both sides. Simultaneously, a critical assessment is present and weak points are identified. The academic analysis of the bilateral relations is combined with concrete measures suggested to overcome the obstacles. Moreover, the experts discussed the perspective and prospective spheres of the cooperation.

The chapter on, "India-Russia Defence Cooperation: Perspectives and Prospects", enumerates that Russia is the biggest defence partner of India with more than 70 to 80 per cent of Indian military's hardware being imported from Russia. The Indo-Russian relationship has now evolved from buyer-seller to co-producer in the fields of design, development and scientific research. The chapter also points out that despite the robust defence relationship, there are notes of dissonance in defence cooperation namely, delays in delivery, lack of transparency, diversification by India, 'friendship prices' no longer being offered by

Russia, supply of sub-standard and inferior ex-stock equipment, doubts about the quality of products, problem of spare parts in upgrading and modernising the equipments. The author concludes by highlighting that India and Russia need to overcome their differences to provide a positive dimension to the long standing relationships. This will not only require a positive attitude but an abiding commitment on the part of both countries.

The chapter on "India-Russia Energy Cooperation" in this book noted the fact that increasing development and urbanisation of India increases the demand for energy, consequently leading to the growth of import dependency of India. In this chapter, the author has tried to show why India needs to look towards Russia for fulfilling India's energy requirements; currently India largely concentrates on West Asia for oil, Qatar for natural gas and Asia Pacific for coal. The chapter emphasises that the diversification of India's energy partners will enable India to fulfil its future energy demands, and highlights that durable energy relations must be seen as part of a larger trade and balanced political relationship. The chapter stressed on the larger geopolitical alignments with regard to energy engagements required for the pragmatic approach to foreign policy. In conclusion, this chapter suggests that though the present energy routes are of utmost importance in the short term, the groundwork for an alternative route is required for leveraging regional frameworks/dialogues for greater energy trade.

In chapter on, "India-Russia Space Cooperation", the author begins by emphasising that both India and Russia have collaborated successfully in various strategic areas of importance, and space is one of them. Russia is the second most potent space power in the world with a wide ranging space programme. Therefore, space presents a realistic opportunity for Indo-Russian cooperation while protecting individual national interests. Bilateral space cooperation is a new beginning for India-Russia bilateral relations. The chapter suggests that collaborating with Russia in the space sector will be fruitful for both the countries. The author here concludes the chapter on a positive note by emphasising that India-Russia could achieve better results within a short span of time if Russia allows India to send humans into space (moon) in the near future; enabling India to emerge as leader in the deep space arena. Russia needs to expand its presence in the global space market, and India could be a reliable partner in this endeavour.

The chapter entitled "Hindrances in Indo-Russian Defence Cooperation" explains that defence cooperation can be frequently regarded as a yardstick for assessing relationships between two countries. This expresses concern over the focus of India's defence cooperation which is restricted to defence acquisitions while its potential in other fields has been neglected. There are inequities in defence procurement which need to be examined. According to the author, apart from the issues of timely provision of even major items as aircraft, ships and submarines, intellectual property rights, transfer of technology and pricing continue to bug this relationship from time to time. The chapter emphasises that there is adequate scope for a broad-based relationship to include joint training and exercises, sharing of experience in counter-terrorism, NBC defence, winter and cold weather warfare, global space navigation system as GLONASS and so on, which has not been fully exposed so far. The author is hopeful that these will facilitate a sharing of Indo-Russian experience in various spheres for mutual benefits so that the strategic relationship is extended into more tangible spheres. The chapter concludes by emphasising the sufficient scope for joint projects with joint production in defence research and development.

The chapter on, "Economic Subsystem of Russia-India Relations", states that both countries are natural and objective friends, sharing similar problems. Geographically, both hold a strategic position in their respective regions. The author is critical about the prospects of trade relations, as geographical factors have continuously played a negative role. The long sea route raises sharply the price of transportation. This chapter maintains that to reduce the cost it will be essential to open up a full-fledged transport corridor, "North-South" (Russia-Iran-India), and make it into a genuine service. There are other economic spheres that have huge developmental potential, especially in the energy sector. The possibilities for cooperation in the fields of atomic energy, heat and power engineering and hydropower engineering, the construction of hydropower railways in India and modernisation of metallurgical works, coal mining and engineering industry are considerable. Here, the author encourages joint ventures. However, the growth of this bilateral economic relationship has to be based on real political will.

The chapter on "Indo-Russian Economic Linkages: A Critical Analysis", observes that after the disintegration of the Soviet Union, the relationship between both the countries has been affected severely. Therefore, despite having good economic and trade relations in the past, the last 15 years have been a period of difficult adjustments, for both Indian and Russian businesses. This chapter points out that bilateral economic relations are surviving mainly because of defence purchases and some public sector investments by India. After the collapse of the USSR, the trade regime was renegotiated and since then, all Russian exports to India have followed the new system. The author noted that in the past, USSR played an important role in India's industrialisation process. It had a relative advantage in sectors like steel, which was central to its requirements. India has to now assess where Russia has a comparative advantage. So far, India has been able to develop linkages with regard to defence production, oil and gas sector and nuclear technology. Indian industry has already identified areas of mutual interest *viz.*, information technology, pharmaceuticals, telecommunications, financial services, hydrocarbons, energy and power, oil and gas, food processing, financial consultancy, management services, textiles and diamond processing. This chapter points out the problematic areas which are well known, including lack of information, visa problems, logistic issues, etc., and regrets that still very little attempt has been made to address them. However, the author is hopeful that the North-South trade corridor will be able to tackle some of the transportation problems. This has not been materialised because of specific reasons. The author comments that while India has signed bilateral trade agreements with various countries, and several are under negotiation, it is still a mystery why the India-Russia free trade deal is nowhere in the horizon.

The chapter on, "Russia and India in a Multi-Dimensional World: An Experiment with Five Indices", discusses the five indices: public, external and internal threats, the capabilities of international influence, quality of life and the institutional foundations of democracy. This objective, theoretical approach shows India in the most favourable light.

Russia, like all countries in transition, has only just started on the road to democracy. The journey ahead is long. Democracy and economic prosperity go hand-in-hand but without grassroots democracy, economic take-off could be delayed, thwarted or warped. Socio-psychological consequences of pauperisation of the society and its property stratification weakens the position of democracy. Even in Europe, the cradle of democracy, the development of democracy was always directly linked to socioeconomic progress. The chapter emphasises that if no action is taken in favour of the socioeconomic recovery and development of Russia, the process of democratisation could be extinguished. In the last part of the chapter, the analyses relies on quantitative rather than qualitative approach, justifying the main conclusion by hard statistical data processed by means of multi-dimensional statistical analysis.

The chapter on the "Strategic Interests of Russia in Asia-Pacific Region" observes that the last decade has changed the foreign policy preferences of Russia. The geographical and strategic location of Russia interlinks itself with two parts of the globe i.e., Europe and Asia. Consequently, Russia's desire for a multipolar world necessitates cooperation with the major regional powers. Here, the author points out that Russia wishes to be part of the East Asian Community, and at the same time is committed to promoting the Russia-India-China *troika*. The author concludes the chapter by emphasising that bilateral and multilateral cooperation should be strengthened further.

The chapter on, "India-Russia Strategic Cooperation: Eye on the Future", examines the diversified relationship between both the countries. Here, the author states that Russia is the major defence partner of India, mentioning various challenges and immense opportunities that exists in this sector. Nevertheless, for improving future cooperation, greater transparency will be needed on Russia's part. There is discussion on trade and economic relations between the countries and here the author expresses the concerns over the low volume of two-way bilateral trade, which according to the author, is much below its true potential. Further, the chapter emphasises that India's energy requirements are increasing rapidly and Russia could play an important role in maintaining India's energy security. There is a vast potential or collaboration in the space sector, particularly in joint research and manufacturing. The author points out the need for increasing people to people contact and information flow between the countries. Amidst all these challenges, there is a discernible continuum in bilateral relations; it is this continuity that provides dynamism and hope that in future, both the countries will exploit mutual strengths and complementarities.

On the whole, optimism is expressed in all the chapters of this volume. Russia's and India's interests have generally tended to coincide whether it is the issue of terrorism, defence or of territorial integrity. There is empathy for each other. Both India and Russia share similar and close geostrategic interests, which provides the basis for their cooperation. Though this does not exclude differences of approach on certain specific issues, the overall parallelism of interests has been evident. The two sides so far have a sympathetic understanding of each other's concerns, even as each retains its autonomy of action. Though after the disintegration of the Soviet Union, this relationship has come under strain, both the countries have worked hard to get back to their old status. There is, however, a need to strengthen the ties further in the near future. It is obvious that India-Russia can play a major role in making the world more stable and safe.

Section I
India-Russia Cooperation in Defence, Space and Energy Sector

1 India-Russia Defence Cooperation

Perspectives and Prospects

Arun Sahgal

Introduction

During the visit of the Russian Defence Minister in October 2008, the two countries agreed to extend the term of the Indo-Russian Inter-Governmental Commission for Military-Technical Cooperation (IRIGC-MTC) for another 10 years—till 2020. Coming at a time when serious dissonance had crept in the Indo-Russian defence ties with possible negative spin-offs on bilateral strategic relationship, the extension of agreement indeed has been a step in the right direction. As a consequence, particular attention is expected to be paid to scientific research and joint development, joint production of systems and platforms and enhanced interaction between the two armed forces. According to Indian Defence Minister Mr. A.K. Antony, Indo-Russian relationship has now reached from buyer-seller to co-producer in the field of design, development and scientific research.

Large number of proposals for joint projects, including the modernisation of the Vikramaditya aircraft carrier (formerly the Admiral Gorshkov) for the Navy, the transfer of technology for the licensed assembly of T-90 tanks in India, the production of BrahMos missiles, the purchase of Smerch Multiple Launch Rocket System (MLRS) and fifth generation fighter which according to Russian sources is scheduled to undertake its first demonstration flight on 12th August 2009 (Russian Air Force Day) were discussed. Also discussed were the lease of Project 971 Shchuka-B Class (NATO designation: Akula-II) nuclear submarines to India for a 10-year lease period. Acknowledgment of such a leasing agreement was for the first time made in January 2009, by the Director of Federal Service for Military-Technical Cooperation, Mikhail Dmitriev when he announced the possibility of Russia transferring these SSN submarines to India.

In recent years, the major weapon systems contracted from Russia include Su-30MKI, a multi-role fighter aircraft, L-78 tanker aircraft to be used as platform for Airborne Warning and Control System (AWACS), Mi-17IV military transport helicopters, R-77 air-to-air missiles, Kilo class/type 877E submarines, stealth frigates, Ka-31 Helix airborne early warning helicopters, aircraft carrier Admiral Gorshkov, MiG-29K, including MiG-29KUB version for use on aircraft carrier and Ka-31 helicopters, T-90 tanks, fire control radar, air and sea surveillance radar, combat radar, aircraft radar, anti-tank and anti-ship missiles besides other assorted military systems and equipment. Recently, the Cabinet committee on security in India also cleared the sale of 80 Mi-17v5 medium transport aircraft and 6 additional IL-78 refuellers among others.

Cooperation in defence constitutes perhaps the most important feature of Indo–Russian bilateral ties. Almost 70 per cent of Indian military hardware is of Soviet and Russian origin and has performed well in all serious military contingencies that India has been involved in. Indeed, cooperation in the sensitive defence sector presupposes and has engendered a high level of mutual trust and broad compatibility of geo-strategic interests and has justifiably been one of the important precepts of bilateral relationship. This is underscored by the fact that energy and defence–military sales are the mainstay, and comprise the bulk of Russian exports.

Looking back at the Indo-Russian defence ties after Independence, India imported large quantity of defence equipment from UK, other European countries and the Soviet Union. In the mid-sixties, the bulk of the imports were from the former Soviet Union. In 1980s, an attempt was made at diversification by import of weapon systems from different sources together with impetus imparted to strengthen own defence industry, especially the defence public sector undertakings, along with attempts to boost indigenous production through increased R&D by Defence Research and Development Organisation (DRDO).

Notwithstanding the above attempts, the bulk of the weapon systems were purchased from the former Soviet Union. There were arrangements with the Soviet Union for something like barter trade, for instance, purchase of defence equipment through Rupee-Rouble arrangements which saved India precious and scarce foreign exchange. Both deferred payments and savings in terms of foreign exchange reduced the adverse impact and heavy financial burden on the defence budget which India was forced to incur in the then prevailing adverse security environment. Also, after importing a specific number of weapon platforms, e.g. Mig-21 jet fighters, licensed production in terms of their assembly was resorted to in India. Further, these arrangements enabled the Indian defence industry to develop its own capacities which were at best limited in the early years of Independence.

Post-Cold War

With the end of the Cold War, Russian defence plants lost nearly 80 per cent of their funding from the Russian government. Simultaneously, there was loss of export earnings due to the loss of traditional Soviet bloc market and the general decline in the world arms market. During the 1990s, the Russian defence budget dropped to levels that were a fraction of the Soviet era, and was manifestly insufficient to support many of the existing defence firms of its vast Military Industrial Complex (MIC), comprising 2000 enterprises, 900 research organisations and design centres with a combined workforce of around five million. Arms exports were seen as crucial to the survival of the vast MIC in the absence or paucity of domestic defence orders. India and China emerged as principal buyers of Russian military equipment.

The main concern of India during this period was to ensure supply of spare parts for the bulk of the Soviet equipment already in its inventory. Several delegations were deputed to scour defence factories of original equipment manufacturers (OEM) scattered all over former Soviet Union literally with suitcases full of money in search of spare parts that were hard to come by.

India understandably, did not buy any new weapons nor were there major arms transfers during this period related to orders given to the former Soviet Union. The fact that Russia buckled under US pressure in

1993 on the issue of cryogenic nuclear deal also created doubts about the reliability of Russia as a defence supplier. However, the fact that Russia did not impose sanctions against India following the 1998 nuclear tests and in fact moved ahead on the Soviet era deal of building two nuclear power plants of 1000 MW capacity at Koodankulam went a long way in rebuilding mutual confidence and resulted in signing in 1998 of the long-term military technical cooperation agreement up to 2010.

It needs to be underscored that this experience of breakup of the former Soviet Union and drying up of primary source of spares and equipment had a deep impact on Indian security planners. As a result of these developments, India was forced to look for alternative sources and this affected the market share of Russian defence industry in India's arms market. Meanwhile, Israeli defence industry, after normalisation of India-Israel relations in 1992, and the European defence companies, captured the marketing space lost by Russia.

Despite the above concerns, however, around the late nineties major defence sales from Russia commenced once again. This period also saw the consolidation of the Russian MIC and renewed investments in design and development.

Prospects and Perspectives

Notwithstanding the confidence reposed in continuing military commerce with Russia, there have been some persistent concerns of India. It needs to be underscored that in any relationship it is important to build mutual confidence and address underlying concerns which could over a period impact otherwise good relations.

Indian armed forces have often complained about persistent problems with spare parts and maintenance support for Russian equipment. Part of the blame can be apportioned onto the Indian negotiators for not visualising and catering for life cycle support while negotiating contractual agreements, including greater wear and tear of the equipment due to varying climatic and operational conditions in India. The harsh fact is that there has been a lack of transparency regarding pricing and low quality of spares; other monopolistic practices have also been a cause of friction. This is further compounded by the fact that some of the equipment imported became obsolete few years after acquisition and closing down of manufacturing plants leading to non-availability of spare parts.

It is not only India which has been complaining on this score. Take the case of Algeria which recently rejected Russian MiG-29 fighter aircraft imports after nearly three years of trying to close a 1.3 billion dollar arms deal. The Algerians cited the "inferior quality" of the fighters and highlighted an even greater symptom of Russian military sales; namely cost overruns, inability to meet delivery timelines, poor production, faulty equipment, unreliable maintenance support, and lack of spare parts and replacement components. India, which has an inventory of nearly three squadrons of Mig-29s, is concerned with structural defects in the planes that could lead to their grounding.

In 2000, the state arms monopoly Rosoboronexport was created to exercise control over almost all the Russian arms exports and supply of spare parts. India has been persistently taking up the issue of product support for equipment of Soviet/Russian origin at the meetings of Indo-Russian Inter-Governmental Commission on Military-Technical Cooperation (IRIGC-MTC). While large numbers of issues have been resolved some problems still persist.

India too faces the dilemma faced by other importers of Russian equipment as highlighted in the case of Algeria. Whereas India does not expect to obtain Russian equipment based on the erstwhile 'friendship prices' of the Soviet era, the increasing tendency to regularly increase prices in the middle of execution of contracts and delay deliveries strikes a negative chord with the Indian planners. Aircraft carrier Admiral Gorshkov, is only one such example among many others. Last year in April, there were intense negotiations between the Ministry of Defence and Russian representatives to ensure that the latter's stand does not delay India's defence modernisation and massive procurement programmes, but then delays were witnessed for one reason or another in almost all major defence deals with Russia, including additional demand as reported in the press.

Timelines set for the supply of Su-30MKI were not met. There were also delays in the upgradation of MiG-21 to the MiG-21-93 level.

Initially, the Su-30MKI aircraft that India imported did not have all the features but the same were provided later, after remonstration with Russians.

Reports from Russia indicate that its defence industrial complex is facing serious problems as Russia attempts to upgrade its technological base to modernise its own defence forces. Some of its key projects are facing severe developmental problems. For example, Russian military has continued to struggle with its advanced Bulava missile. Its most recent launch on December 23, 2008 resulted in self-destruction during its flight. This test marked the fifth failure out of a total of 10 launches. Similar is the case of Russian fifth generation fighter aircrafts. While there is a sense of optimism surrounding the new fighter, military analysts in Russia, however, note that fifth generation aircrafts are really fourth generation fighters with upgraded avionics. One of the important elements that denotes a fifth generation fighter, namely stealth, is not seen with the SU-35, which has 22 square metres of reflecting radar surface *versus* the United States Air Force's F-22 Raptor with a reflecting surface of 0.003 square metres. Another Russian Defence Ministry expert source points out that many of the modifications to the Russian fighters (MiG-35 or the Su-35) are primarily designed to assist in extending the lifespan of these aircrafts and that Russia's fifth generation fighter programme has "largely remained on paper". Hardly the stuff which can impose confidence in prospective buyers. Then there is the case of MiG-29 discussed earlier. Other problems include the ageing Russian defence industrial workforce, slumping oil prices, and increasing costs of raw materials. For example, the price of nickel alloys has increased despite an overall reduction in demand. This is forcing Soviet industrial planners and political planners to seek leasing and joint production as routes to defray costs and remain competitive.

Quality of Spares

Another negative feature of the defence relationship has been the indifferent quality of the equipment supplied at times. During the Kargil war of 1999, the majority of the Krasnopol precision-guided munition was found to be defective. Similarly, other equipments like T-90s was handed over to India without some of the necessary weapons like missile firing systems. In case of Tunguska Air Defence System, old and rusted systems were initially provided and replaced after protracted and taxing negotiations.

As mentioned, these hiccups have not deterred India from enhancing its military technical cooperation with Russia because of two principal reasons. One, massive requirements of the Indian armed forces in pursuance of attaining the goals of 'Revolution in Military Affairs' in an early time frame, and the fact that the majority of the equipment was of erstwhile Soviet origin. Second, there is an abiding faith in the robustness and functional efficacy of the Russian equipment which has proved its mettle in many conflicts. It will not be wrong to say that India has perhaps been the best proving ground of Russian equipment and advertiser of its versatility.

This is further underscored by the fact that in October 2007, India and Russia signed a pact on jointly developing and producing a fifth generation combat aircraft in addition to reaching an understanding on the contentious price escalation issue over the purchase of 40 additional Sukhoi Su-30 fighters for the Indian Air Force. The fifth generation fighter MiG-35 is expected to be in the same class as F-22 (Raptor) and F-35 Joint Strike Fighter (JSF) of the US. However, as highlighted above, concerns voiced in Russia with regard to the fifth generation programme particularly its 'stealth' features could force India to rethink its options despite massive cost differential. In addition, in November 2007 both governments signed an agreement for joint development and production of IL-214 multi-role transport aircraft (MTA).

This long-planned Russian-Indian MTA project will bring to life a next-generation tactical airlifter with a maximum payload capability of 20 tonnes. New Delhi has agreed to directly invest $300 million for work to be done by Hindustan Aeronautics Limited (HAL). It would phase out the ageing Soviet-built Antonov An-24 and An-32 aircraft from the air forces of both nations. Further, both countries have reached an agreement on the use of Russia's global space navigation system. Global Navigation Satellite System (GLONASS), a Russian version of the US Global Positioning System (GPS), designed for both military and civilian purposes is likely to become fully functional by 2011, allowing users to identify their positions in real time. Here again it needs to be mentioned, reports emanating from Russia (see *The Institute of Study of Conflict Ideology and Policy Analyst* XV(8), 19 February 2009) are not encouraging. There are reports of satellite malfunction and frequent closures for maintenance.

An existing success story, however is that of the joint enterprise Brahmos Ltd. which manufactures state-of-the-art cruise missiles suitable for land, sea and air based launch platforms. The project seems to have met with considerable success. During a defence exhibition held in Indonesia (Indo Defence 2006 Expo and Forum), marketing initiatives of BrahMos clearly overshadowed all of the Russian missile exhibitors.

Changing Perspective of Arms Acquisition

While Russia enjoyed virtual monopoly in the Indian market back in the 70s, 80s and early 90s, India in the recent years has taken a conscious decision to diversify its sources of arms procurement and link these with the broader perspective of developing an indigenous defence industrial base. It needs to be noted that India has moved into alternate sourcing, particularly Israel and France in segments where Russia is relatively weak. These include electronic and electro optic systems, electronic warfare (EW) and info technologies, command and communication systems, unmanned aerial vehicles (UAVs) and non-nuclear submarines with air-independent propulsion systems.

There appear to be some concerns about the likelihood of big entry of the United States in the Indian arms market with attempts to improve their market share to 20-25 per cent. The point to note is that firstly, the majority of US equipment will relate to support rather than combat system. The only exception perhaps could be open tender bid of Multi-Role Combat Aircraft (MRCA). This will of course depend upon detailed, technical evaluation and commercial negotiations, apart of course from political factors.

Here, two issues merit attention. One, India is consciously embarking upon creating indigenous defence R&D and industrial base. Towards this, an attempt is being made to source sophisticated state-of-the-art technologies together with transfer of technology being built into all major contracts. This is being done through an offset programme which will form part of all major defence contracts as per new defence procurement policy. So far, in contracts with Russia, the above provisions have not been invoked. However, these will certainly be a part of future contracts and will have to be complied within a competitive bidding environment.

The second issue which is specific to Indo-Russian defence cooperation is the degree and nature of shift from licensed to joint projects based exclusively on financial and technological investments and risk sharing. This is seen as a win-win situation for three specific reasons: one, Russia has technological expertise in the two areas of joint development *viz.*, MiG–35 and MTA, second there are little or no political risks to such cooperation and lastly, from Indian perspective, development of Indian Military Industrial Complex (MIC) should be seen in the interest of both the countries.

It needs to be recognised that in terms of transfer of technology and contracts for many a front line equipment such as aircrafts, helicopters, artillery guns, radars etc., India's options today are far greater than before. Nonetheless, India is aware that countries are unlikely to part with the state-of-the-art technologies without a price in some form or the other. Some strategic technologies may not be parted with at all. Even though India has signed an Intellectual Property Rights (IPR) agreement with Russia, it is unlikely that some of the cutting edge technologies would be given to India unless there is a broader understanding at the political level. Most of the time, defence deals in high-end technology products are likely to be politico-strategic in nature, and the price may not be the only consideration.

Further, as mentioned earlier India's efforts over the last few years have been directed at improving its procurement procedures, give impetus to indigenous industry and research and development in order to meet its military modernisation objectives. Defence Procurement Procedure-2008 (DPP) along with the offset clause is the latest in the series. The offset clause is to enable transfer of technology, joint production and co-development, and improve indigenous capacity and become self-reliant in the long run. India's claims to become a major power would be of no avail unless it has its own robust and vibrant defence industry.

Intellectual Property Rights (IPR) Agreement

India signed the formal IPR agreement in December 2005 during the Indian Prime Minister's visit to Russia. Nonetheless, events leading to signing of the IPR agreement did create some misunderstanding and heartburning. While Russian insistence on protecting high-end technologies that it shares with India is well appreciated, but despite the signing of the agreement there have been instances of technology denial which have not gone down well. Smerch Multi-barrel Rocket (SMR) system is a case in point. Not only has the technology not been provided but the order itself was scaled down from 69 to 46. Another issue is insistence on mentioning the functioning of the IPR agreement of Russia as the preferred supplier, a provision, against which number of analysts have cautioned. Though India has reportedly accepted this provision given its continuing dependence on Russian arms supplies, there is a need to iron out differences and create a level playing field for mutual benefit.

It needs to be underscored that Russian arms exports are down to $6 billion in 2007-08 from $8 billion in the previous year. With the economic downturn facing the world, these sales are likely to plunge. It is important therefore, to have a level playing field and ensure an equitable relationship. In terms of arms sales it may be worthwhile to point out the Russian experience with the Chinese to whom sales in 2007-08 have shown a perceptible downturn. There are also rumours of a serious feud between Russian manufacturers and the Chinese over stolen technology. What is worse, the Chinese have been most brazen about not only copying Russian technology but, exporting it as well. The point being highlighted is that despite differences, India has played by the rules. In the face of current controversies, this aspect assumes additional relevance.

Indo–Russian Military to Military Cooperation

The facet of military to military cooperation is gaining ground between the two countries. Indo–Russian defence cooperation has largely been in the military technical field. This taboo was recently broken with both countries stepping up joint exercises. In October 2005, the two armies held joint exercises in the deserts of Rajasthan. For the first time these were followed by naval exercises off the coast of Visakhapatnam and exercises between Special Forces of the two countries. Ironically, while India has been engaging regularly with US, European and Asian nations in joint manoeuvres and exercises, there has been certain degree of reticence between India and Russia.

Given the fact that India and Russia have a long history of successful defence relationship, frequent exercises and joint seminars are important for building up a good military relationship, as well as sharing concepts and doctrines, and above all, building mutual trust. While it is appreciated that language could be a barrier, however, this issue can be overcome in a manner similar to joint exercises with China under the rubric of Shanghai Cooperation Organisation (SCO). It is our considered view that there is a need to provide positive dimension to the overall relationship between the two old strategic partners.

Conclusion

In terms of defence procurement relationship, while no doubt Russia will remain a major partner for India in the coming few decades, the Russian industry too needs to learn to compete with the West, the Israelis and the fast upcoming indigenous defence industry, as it goes about broad-basing its defence procurement and creating indigenous capacities. The fact remains that the defence market today, leaving out certain high-end technologies, is a buyer's market and that India is one of the largest defence importers in the world. Indian efforts would be directed towards leveraging this position for maximising benefits including developing its own capacities.

India and Russia need to overcome whatever differences there are and provide a positive dimension to this long standing relationship. This will not only require a positive attitude but an abiding commitment on the part of both countries.

References

Bakshi, Jyotsna (2006). "India-Russia defence cooperation", *Strategic Analysis* 30(2), April-June, Institute for Defence Studies and Analysis.

Business Standard (2009). "Defective defence equipment a concern for Indo-Russia ties", *Business Standard*, March 17, Delhi.

IANS (2008). *India, Russia to Extend Military Cooperation Beyond 2010*. September 29.

Menon, Narayan (2008). "India-Russia strategic relations", *Indian Defence Review* 23(1).

Moscow Defense Brief (2008). "Russia arms trade in the first half of 2008", *Moscow Defense Brief* 3(13).

———. (2008). "Russia-India military-technical cooperation: Current issues and perspectives", *Moscow Defense Brief* 4(14).

Start for Analysis (2009). "Russian Defence Industry", *Start for Analysis*, 11 February.

———. (2008). "India: The US – Russian tug-of-war continues", *Start for Analysis*, February 26.

———. (2007). "Military: India's Russian Problem", *Start for Analysis*, December 4.

———. (2005). "Russia–India: Unparalleled cooperation in sensitive areas", *Start for Analysis*, December 5.

The Institute of Study of Conflict Ideology and Policy Analyst XV(8), 19 February 2009.

The Institute of Study of Conflict Ideology and Policy Analyst XV(9), 5 March 2009.

Interviews and discussions with serving and retired military officers and officials.

2 Indo-Russian Space Cooperation

Ajey Lele

The Earth's first artificial satellite, Sputnik, was launched by the erstwhile Soviet Union on October 4, 1957. Since then nation-states have made remarkable progress in the space arena and attained great heights. Americans took only 12 years to reach the moon after the launch of the first satellite by the erstwhile USSR, with their astronauts walking on the surface of the moon for the first time in 1969.

Now for more than five decades, space technologies are encompassing a range of activities, from fundamental research to advanced technology development. These technologies have played a major role in areas like meteorology, communication, navigation, remote sensing and resource management. Space technologies have contributed immensely towards education and research on astronomy. Presently space commerce is showing signs of maturing.

"The beginning of space age in the USSR was not a chance event. On one hand, it was a response to the essence of a totalitarian system based on ideological dogma, a command economy, a powerful military and the lofty ambitions of the Communist party leaders. Together these elements strongly articulated the development of rocketry and propulsion technology as well as many other branches of the military industry."[1] The Soviet Union's launch of 'Sputnik' had kicked off a decade-long 'space race' between the Soviet and the United States. During the Cold War era, Ronald Reagan unfolded a very ambitious programme called the Strategic Defence Initiative (SDI), more commonly known as Star Wars. With the end of Cold War, this one upmanship in space appears to have ended.

Space technologies are expensive, and they put huge demands on the state's financial and infrastructural requirements. Naturally, all these years the discovery of space has remained in the hands of developed and a few developing but technologically savvy nations. However, over the years even the developed West has realised that space exploration is a long-term and ambitious endeavour, and no state can alone embark on it. As a result, in the post-Cold War era, various developments in space arena have essentially been the result of global and international cooperation. The International Space Station (ISS), a research facility currently being assembled in space, is an excellent example of such collaborative efforts where 16 states have joined hands. Today, the ISS has been continuously inhabited since November 2002 with a permanent human presence in space.

During the last few years, Indo-Russian ties, particularly in the field of technology, are showing fresh reverberation. A declaration on strategic partnership was signed between Mr. Vladimir Vladimirovich Putin and Mr. Atal Bihari Vajpayee during October 2000. Both the states are collaborating with each other in various important fields in the space arena. The recent history of cooperation in space between India and Russia is an example of how a developed space power and an emerging space power can work together and lead to the successful realisation of various space technologies related endeavours.

This chapter outlines various aspects of Indo-Russian cooperation in the space arena and attempts to evaluate the strategic and commercial aspects of this cooperation. The chapter restricts itself mainly to discussing a few recent initiatives; it does not attempt to analyse space cooperation between them over the years.

Indo-USSR Space Cooperation: A Historical Narrative

Since the early 1950s, New Delhi and Moscow had built friendly relations on the basis of real politic. The then Prime Minister of India, Pt. Jawaharlal Nehru, undertook his first official visit to the USSR during June 1955 and this could be said to have launched a relationship of mutual respect and trust. It could be said to have started with a major thrust on industrial collaboration. During 1955-56, the Soviet

Union constructed a metallurgical plant in the city of Bhilainagar. The active military-technological cooperation could be said to have started with the Indian government purchasing a large batch of Soviet planes and helicopters for the Air Force during August 1962. The cooperation further expanded with the delivery of T-54 tanks to the Indian army, and the first submarine to its Navy[2], during 1966-67.

The collaboration in the area of space began a bit late mainly because India was yet to conceptualise its space agenda. The first launch from India's Thumba equatorial launch site took place in November 1963; it was a UN sponsored international effort. In these early years of development, the Indian approach was to be open to international cooperation. The first decade saw India launching sounding rockets of American, British, French and Soviet design. India's first satellite, Aryabhatta, was launched on April 19, 1975 on a Soviet Kosmos-3M rocket from a Soviet launch site (Kapustin Yar range). May be by taking help from the USSR for this launch India, being a member of NAM (Non Aligned Movement), was trying to balance its earlier cooperation with the US in this field.[3] The second satellite, Bhaskara-1 for Earth observation, was also launched from Kapustin Yar in 1979. That satellite experienced operational problems too, and was followed by the Bhaskara-II in 1981.[4] During 1977, Indian Space Research Organisation (ISRO) was helped to build an experimental laser based optical.[5] Sqn. Ldr. Rakesh Sharma, India's only cosmonaut, visited space on board Soyuz T-10 (1984). For India, this was more for political prestige than practical benefit. This move by the USSR, of sending an Indian into space, not only boosted India's image but also made its people proud of the achievement. There was no further collaboration in any major areas related to space exploration.

Russia-India Space Voyage

Despite the disintegration of the USSR, the relationship between India and Russia remains one of considerable importance to both countries. They have collaborated in various strategic areas for the last two decades and space is one of them. Presently, Russia is the second most potent space power in the world. It considers space as a "strategic resource" and uses it to meet its social obligations and enhancing its national security.

The majority of former Soviet space facilities and expertise is concentrated in Russia.[6] The country has a wide ranging space programme and its space policy is governed by the 1993 security doctrine.[7]

The Russian space journey could be said to be marred by various ups and downs during the last two decades. The progress during last few years indicates that probably post-Cold War, Russia took a conscious decision to come out of its 'confidentiality syndrome' with regard to its space activities. Since 1993, it has been participating in various international space programmes. During the initial years post disintegration, Russia as a state underwent considerable turmoil and this got reflected in its space policies.[8] Due to budgetary constraints, the state was not left with much of a choice but to look for global participation for the 'survival' of its space agenda. However, the capacity of Russia to generate new technology has always been highly appreciated. During the period 1989-2002, state support for space activities declined by almost 20 times. The space expenditures of GNP declined from 0.73 per cent in 1989 to 0.1 per cent in 1998.[9] However, Putin played a major role towards bringing space back to the centre of the 'strategic and economic' agenda of the country.

On the other hand, India had a modest beginning in the space arena. For India, space technology was a tool catering to its model of socio-economic development. As mentioned earlier, the Indian space programme has evolved as a combination of internal expertise and international collaborations. In regard to international collaboration, there were no biases in the selection of a state for bilateral arrangements. India had taken help from the US, France, the UK and erstwhile USSR. However, during the last few decades the Indian space programme has experienced exponential growth and is currently being recognised for its professionalism all over the world. In the year 2008, India had also entered into the arena of deep space missions.

Due to the technological semblance between space launch vehicles and ballistic missiles, technology transfer in the launch vehicle arena is always looked with suspicion all over the world. In order to avoid any wrongful proliferation of technology, global norms have been established in regard to technology transfer. At times these norms are used with extreme caution, some times even to covertly achieve the political agenda of a particular nation. India-Russia space cooperation could be said to be a victim of such geopolitical realities. In 1992, the US objected to an agreement between the Glavkosmos and ISRO for the sale of cryogenic rocket engines to India and the technology to produce them. The contract also included transfer of technology. The US believed such exports violated the rules of the Missile Technology Control Regime (MTCR).[10] They felt cryogenic units employed on space launch vehicles might contribute to India's development of the top stage of a missile above the MTCR threshold. The suspension of 1993 cryogenic deal had multiple ramifications for India's GSLV (Geosynchronous Satellite Launch Vehicles) programme and it could be said that it gave a major setback to India's space ambitions and delayed its programme significantly. Unilateral termination of cryogenic engine contract by Russia had a considerable negative impact on Indo-Russian relations not only in space arena but even in regard to overall relations.

Subsequently, the agreement was renegotiated and Russia committed seven fully assembled KVD-1 engines (no technology transfer). India has also started the indigenous development process of cryogenic engines. However, this is a huge technological challenge and after so many years it is only now that India's efforts are close to achieving fruition in this field. India has decided to integrate all seven GSLV Mk. I launchers with upper stages powered by Russian KVD-1 rocket motors and use indigenous engines in future versions of the GSLV Mk. II.[11]

India carried out its second nuclear test during 1998 (Pokharan-II). This test was seen as defiance of the global nuclear disarmament architecture and India was put under sanctions. Naturally, Pokharan-II played a significant role in amplifying India's technological apartheid which had an adverse impact on India's space programme. Technological agreements in the defence and space arena essentially dried up, mainly with the US and other European powers. Over a period of time, the revival of Indo-Russian military ties has taken place; but this was more driven by economic factors.[12]

Space Cooperation: A New Beginning

Overcoming the various setbacks because of international flip-flop on technology transfer policies by the beginning of 21st century, India demonstrated that its 'space rendezvous' may have got delayed, but could not be derailed. India achieved stupendous success in the field of remote sensing and transponder technology, and has also successfully carved a place for itself in the global commercial space market. This century offers many realistic opportunities for Indo-Russia cooperation.

The century started with India launching the GSAT-1 communication satellite by using Russian made KVD-1 cryogenic upper stage onboard GSLV Mk. I launcher. However, in this century cooperation is expected to go much beyond the 'launch vehicle' assistance. Both the states understand that they can cooperate with each other in this field while protecting individual national interests. Today, both countries are aware of the need for cooperation. The last decade was difficult for Russia to continue with its space agenda because of economic constraints. Declining budgets was one reason why it was looking for international collaborators in this field. For the Russians, India was a natural choice. India was no longer regarded as a pariah. On the Indian front also, there was need to work with a reliable partner who could offer the requisite assistance with regard to technology.

The Indo-Russian space cooperation started in the post-Cold War era with the signing of an agreement in 1994 between ISRO and the Russian Space Agency. An umbrella agreement, signed at the government level in 2004, has given a further boost to this relationship. The major thrust could be said to have been with regard to collaboration over the GLONASS (Global Orbiting Navigation Satellite System), collaboration in the project 'Youth Satellite', and participation in India's 'moon mission'. These above collaborations in the space arena, in recent times is elaborated as under.

GLONASS

India and Russia have reached an agreement on the access to navigation, a signal of the GLONASS for peaceful purposes and also as per this agreement, India has become a part of the GLONASS Radio Frequency

Spectrum. In fact, GLONASS is an old system that came into being in 1976. The first GLONASS satellite was launched into orbit in 1982, but the system became operational only in 1995. This satellite constellation is a Russian version of the US Global Positioning System (GPS) and the European Galileo system. It is designed for both military and civilian purposes, and allows users to identify their positions in real time. It can also be used in geological prospecting, air traffic control, mobile telephony, sensor technology and police surveillance. These satellites operate in circular orbits (19,100 km above ground) and offer accuracy for civilian users up to 30 metres.

Currently, the Russian system in space constitutes a few old GLONASS series satellites and more than half a dozen satellites of the GLONASS-M series, launched after 2004, with a working life period of seven years. The GLONASS-K would be next generation series with lighter weights and a 10-12 year life span. Under this agreement, Russia and India plan to jointly use GLONASS.[13] As of March 2009, a total of 20 satellites are operational in orbit for military and civilian purposes.[14] In 2008, Russia has taken a decision to raise the production of GLONASS sets to increase the vast market of users. By the end of 2009, the system is expected to have 24 operational satellites in the orbit. The Russians are even talking with the US and the European Space Agency on using GLONASS jointly with GPS and the Galileo satellite navigation systems.

India's interests in GLONASS do have a military angle as well. Today India's major military hardware is of Russian origin; and GLONASS would naturally offer a compatible navigation solution. In any case, the GPS and Galileo do not offer military applications to its commercial users. Therefore, over time, India is expected to have larger stakes in GLONASS, and could be involved in production and joint use as partners. Particularly for India, both for civil and military aviation, there is an urgent need to have a global positioning system.

For India, GLONASS collaboration means an end of its dependence on GPS. Also, India's earlier proposal to have collaboration with the European system, Galileo, has not worked out. India is expected to purchase 126 multi-role combat aircrafts in the near future and has also tied-up with Russia for joint venture on fifth generation fighter aircraft. The availability of GLONASS would play a crucial role in deciding the might of India's aerospace power in this century. For India, satellite navigation has got strategic relevance, and is also aware of the fact that Russia has refused to part with this technology to China.

YouthSat

India would be launching a dedicated satellite for the youth during 2009. The satellite would carry scientific instruments developed by students from Indian and foreign universities. A mini-spacecraft will be launched in 2009 as a piggyback on board a polar satellite launch vehicle (PSLV), carrying a remote sensing satellite, from the Satish Dhawan Space Centre at Sriharikota (about 90 km from Chennai). The various instruments, developed by graduate and postgraduate students of universities from India, Russia and other countries, will study and share data on earth imaging, atmospheric applications, solar emission and galactic observations.

This less than 100-kg spacecraft is being built at India's satellite development centre in Bangalore. The dedicated youth satellite is the brainchild of former president A.P.J. Abdul Kalam, who proposed such a mission during his visit to Russia a few years ago. As an auxiliary satellite, it will be a dedicated platform for aerospace students to conduct experiments, which will also give some idea about the coupling between sun and earth. This mini-satellite would be christened YouthSat. The purpose here is to create a common platform for aerospace students across the world to jointly conduct experiments in space for the benefit of future generations and humanity as a whole.

India feels that there is a need to impress upon the modern youth to take up studies in rocket science. It is envisaged that YouthSat could motivate the younger generation towards 'space research'. There is also a need to take Indo-Russia space collaboration and research beyond the official level by involving civil society. Moreover, this satellite will enable India to test the cost-effective options for outer space research; with this launch India would make a fresh beginning in the 21st century towards investing into atmospheric research.

Chandrayaan-2

India has already successfully launched its first moon mission Chandrayaan-1 in the year 2008. This probe is expected to revolve around the moon for an approximate period of 18 months. India is partnering Russia for its second moon mission called Chandrayaan-2. For this mission, both the states would share work. ISRO and Russia's Federal Space Agency, Roscosmos, have signed an agreement to that effect for a joint lunar research and exploration mission. India's second moon mission is expected to take place during 2010-11.

The role of both the parties have also been clearly spelled out. Chandrayaan-2 mission will consist of a spacecraft and a landing platform with the moon rover. The platform with the rover will detach itself after the spacecraft reaches its orbit above the moon and lands on lunar soil. ISRO will be responsible for the orbiter and Russia for the moon rover. The rover would remain functional for a month. It will be programmed to pick up soil and rock samples and would immediately carry out its chemical analysis. This valuable data will, in turn, be transmitted to the spacecraft orbiting above the moon. The weight of the rover would depend on the nature of the landing envisaged. It could be anywhere between 30-100 kg.[15]

For India it is very important to collaborate with Russia in this field because of Russia's experience with deep space missions. India expects that both states could effectively carry out mineral and chemical mapping of the moon surface which has relevance in regard to energy security (availability of Helium-3 on the surface of the moon could change the global energy scenario enormously). India also understands that the spin-off technologies developed during this mission could have both civil and military relevance.

Other Missions

Indian and Russian space agencies have agreed on cooperation in the field of solar physics and solar-terrestrial relationships within the framework of the Coronas-Photon Project.[16] The Tata Institute of Fundamental Research (TIFR) would be supplying a low energy gamma ray telescope for the Russian spacecraft to study solar physics. India has taken Russia's help for the launch of Indian Remote Sensing Satellite (IRS 1C) from Bikaner during 1995. Also, as mentioned earlier, the GSLV launches during 2001, 2003, 2004, 2006 and 2007 had used Russian cryogenic stage technology.

It is also expected that India and Russia will collaborate in few other areas related to space activities in years to come.

Conclusion

The history of India-Russia space cooperation proves that successful and effective joint work is possible in future and several other space related projects at different levels can be undertaken. Both the states could work together more in the arena of deep space missions; an agreement on joint Mars Mission could be a right step in that direction.

In this era of economic meltdown, it is important to understand that heavy budget requirements for space research may not allow both the states to go 'solo' in this field, and bilateral research and development could offer them additional and quick dividends. Russia could also help India to send humans into space. India and Russia together could work towards exploiting the commercial aspects of space navigation (India also proposes to have its own regional navigational system in the near future. GLONASS and this system could together offer a viable commercial package).

Russia needs to expand its presence in the global space market, and India could be a reliable partner in this endeavour. Disarmament is one area where both states need to work together towards the formulation of a globally acceptable space regime. The geopolitics of the 21st century dictate that there is a need to take Indo-Russian collaboration to greater heights and space collaboration could play a key role towards this end.

End Notes

1. Marov, Mikhail Ya. (1992). "The new challenges for space in Russia", *Space Policy* 8(3): 269. August.
2. *http://www.axisglobe.com/article.asp?article=64.* Accessed on September 12, 2008.
3. Sheehan, Michael (2007). *The International Politics of Space.* New York: Routledge. pp.146-147.
4. Barabanov, Mikhail (2008). "Russian-Indian cooperation in space", *Moscow Defense Brief, http://mdb.cast.ru/mdb/1-2005/space/russian_indian/?form=print*, Accessed on December 15.
5. Navalgund, R.R. and K. Kasturirangan (2009). "The Indian remote sensing satellite: A programme overview", *Sadhana* 6(4): 313-336 and Satellite Tracking & Ranging Station (STARS), *http://en.wikipedia.org/wiki/Indian_Space_Research_Organisation*, Accessed on January 12, 2009.
6. Marov, *op.cit*.
7. The 1993 "Basic Provisions of the Russian Federation Military Doctrine" is considered as the basic document and was improvised in 1999 and the draft for the same is available at *http://www.fas.org/nuke/guide/russia/doctrine/991009-draft-doctrine.htm*, Accessed on September 14, 2008.
8. For more on this, please refer Tarasenko, Maxim V. (1996). "Current status of the Russian space programme", *Space Policy* 12 (1): 19-28, February.
9. Pankova, Lyudmila (2002). "Transfer of space technologies past and present: The Russian case", *The Journal of Technology Transfer* 27(4): 349-360, December.
10. Normally MTCR threshold is about weight of missile/range of missile ratio and is expected to be 500 kg/300km.
11. Barabanov, Mikhail (2008). "Russian-Indian cooperation in space", *Moscow Defense Brief, http://mdb.cast.ru/mdb/1-2005/space/russian_indian/?form=print*, Accessed on December 15.
12. Conley, Jerome M. (2000). "Indo-Russian military and nuclear cooperation: Implications for U.S. security interests", *INSS Occasional Paper* 31, *Proliferation Series*, February. Colorado: USAF Institute for National Security Studies.
13. *The Indian Express* (2009). "Watch this Indo-Russia space", January 30.
14. *http://www.glonass-ianc.rsa.ru/pls/htmldb/f?p=202:20:14637162736231801312::NO,* Accessed on March 6, 2009.
15. *The Indian Express* (2007). "A piece of the moon", November 24.
16. For more on this project and study on solar hard radiation, please refer *www.adsabs.harvard.edu/abs/2004cosp.meet,* Accessed on January 15, 2009.

3 Hindrances in Indo-Russian Defence Cooperation

Rahul K. Bhonsle

India and Russia have been strategic partners over the past many decades. The friendship has stood the test of time and weathered many a crisis over the years and has seen an enduring success of foreign policy of both the nations. Defence cooperation can be frequently regarded as a yardstick for assessing relationship between two states. Indo-Russian cooperation in the defence sector in some ways exceeds expectations in this exacting sphere. There are many benchmarks in this field which transcends all the three services to include MiG and Sukhoi fighter induction programmes, submarine and frigates, leasing of Chakra and the T series of tanks for the army. The joint development project, BrahMos, is a seminal achievement in this sphere. This denotes a substantive relationship over an extended period.

Yet, the focus of Indo-Russian defence cooperation has been restricted to defence acquisitions and other fields with potential, such as exercises, training and research and development, which have been neglected. There are inequities in defence procurement as well, which needs to be examined. Moreover, the process seems to be one way; with development of India's defence sector, there is scope for expansion of the relationship. Thus, a realistic appraisal of Indo-Russian cooperation in the defence sector is called for to identify and overcome the hindrances and partake opportunities in the future.

Aim and Scope

The aim of this chapter is to provide an overview of hindrances in Indo-Russian defence cooperation and suggest measures to overcome the same. Given that the chapter forms a part of a series of inter-connected issues in Indo-Russian relations, the focus is on examining hindrances in defence relations. The chapter, thus, covers a broad gamut of issues to include the following main themes:

1. Overview of Indo-Russian Defence Cooperation.
2. Basic Factors Leading to Hindrances.
3. Operative Hindrances–Past and Present.
4. Considerations for Overcoming Hindrances.

Overview of Indo-Russian Defence Cooperation

Broadly speaking, defence ties between India and Russia continue to be robust. Moscow has not surrendered any of the advantages that it had of supplying platforms to New Delhi. It would continue to maintain this primacy in the years ahead as Russia maintains its lead in providing robust, reliable and cost-effective tanks, ships, aircrafts and helicopters. However, there is scope for greater cooperation which needs to be explored by both sides for mutual benefit.

From the Indian perspective, defence cooperation covers a number of parallel activities to include high level defence visits and dialogues, port calls, training exchanges, exercises, sourcing, development, joint production and marketing of military equipment and mutual assistance.[1] The Russian view is not dissimilar and includes joint solution of defence problems, dialogues and interactions at the political, strategic and technical levels.[2]

A review of the defence relationship between India and Russia reveals that it is primarily structured around defence acquisitions. The result of this unitary focus is evident with over 50 per cent of equipment fielded by the Indian armed forces being of Russian/Soviet origin. While this remains an important component of overall strategic relationship, there are issues of dependency, technology redundancy, spares and ancillary support and so on, which came into focus with the collapse of the Soviet Union in 1991. While India supported the Russian defence industry during the critical period, want of spares impacted operational preparedness of the armed forces. This apart, issues of timely provision of even major platforms as aircrafts, ships and submarines, intellectual property rights, transfer of technology and pricing continue to bug this relationship from time to time, the aircraft carrier INS Vikramaditya or Gorshkov being the most salient example of this malaise.

Moreover, there is adequate scope for broad-basing the relationship to include joint training and exercises, sharing of experience in counter terrorism, NBC defence, winter and cold weather warfare, operating navigation systems as GLONASS and so on; these options have not been fully explored so far. This would facilitate sharing of the Indo-Russian experience in various spheres for mutual benefit and extend the strategic relationship into more tangible spheres.

Basic Factors Leading to Hindrances

Defence cooperation is a part of the overall relationships between two nations. The hierarchy of military collaboration is represented by a ladder in descending order as given below:

1. Mutual aid and assistance.
2. Strategic partnership—Common goal.
3. Strategic relationship—Common purpose.
4. Cooperation with or without legacy.
5. Cooperation on a case to case basis.[3]

At the highest level of military to military relations is a compact for mutual aid and assistance. This treaty denotes that the two nations will deter and defend aggression on each other and provide maximum help if the necessity so arises. As the possibility of territorial wars has reduced, this level of cooperation has lost its relevance to a great extent, given that it fell in the paradigm of collective or common security drawn from the Cold War. At the second tier, is strategic partnership where two nations would have a common goal and therefore will adopt parallel and interrelated pathways of cooperation to achieve that goal. At the next level is strategic relationship which indicates a common purpose, though the goals that each nation or armed forces are trying to attain may be different.

Nations and armed forces would also have consistent policies for defence cooperation based on a legacy of the past or worked out in the light of common contemporary challenges. At the lowest level, is cooperation on a case to case basis such as for specific requirements or purpose which is restricted, based on a given time, geographic area or defence domain. For instance, the Indian and the Chinese navies may well decide to cooperate in combating the common challenge faced due to piracy in the Gulf of Aden. This would, thus, be episodic cooperation which may or may not be continued once the common threat has withered away or the Chinese navy has retracted from the Gulf.[4]

The level of cooperation between two states vary, depending on strategic needs, commonality of aims and objectives, and symmetry in capabilities or national power. Where common strategic needs are identified, a treaty of mutual aid and assistance will be worked out while at other times strategic cooperation on a case to case basis would suffice. Russia and India have great consistency in maintaining close defence cooperation impacted by all the three factors stated above. Moreover, both India and Russia are seen to be rising powers in the global political spectrum, with the latter regaining some of its past influence. Based on this general paradigm, Indian and Russian defence cooperation has varied between that of mutual aid and assistance, as signified by the Indo-Soviet Treaty of Peace and Friendship, to that of strategic partnership today.[5]

Given these issues, some of the hindrances seen over the past few years in Indo-Russian defence relationship arise from a number of factors such as lack of a common military legacy and political uncertainties. The Indian armed forces follow the British military pattern, which is alien to the Russians drawn from the legacy of the Red Army. Certain basic issues such as conscription, which is prevalent in the Russian armed forces to this day, and the all volunteer nature of the Indian military, highlights the differences. While both armed forces have a creditable past record going back to the two World Wars, the lack of common standards and culture has perhaps affected their developing close ties. Language is another key barrier, for while English is a common language for the Indian officer community, the level of learning Russian language has gradually come down over the years.

At another level, Indian defence relationship is expanding from a bipolar one with Russia to a multipolar one with the United States, UK,

France, Israel and so on.[6] In this multipolar environment, strategic partnership is difficult to attain, given that interests of the two parties may clash at a given point of time. Thus, there is a natural tendency for dilution of the strategic cooperation. However, so far with concerted efforts and the legacy of past association, this downgradation has not taken place in Indo-Russian relations.

Political uncertainties have been another factor which have hindered smooth defence relations between India and Russia. The period of ambiguity in the pre-Putin period in Russia was a major factor for delays when no firm direction to Russian policies was forthcoming. There were some uncertainties in India from 1996 to 1999 as well, when a clear cut foreign policy had not been enunciated. While such periods were of a limited duration, they adversely affected relations.[7] The financial health of the countries and currencies as well as supplier firms, also had a negative impact. With the collapse of the Soviet Union, the division of the production base in different states created problems of spares which had brought down operational efficiency of the Indian armed forces. This in turn led to considerable apprehensions in the later years on the reliability of source of supply contributing to lack of trust. Today all these issues seem to be a thing of the past, but the 1990s created major discontinuities in defence relations between the two states.[8]

Despite these factors, the level of cooperation throughout the years has been high and focused on defence technology, technology transfer, continued joint and combined exercises, training for officers in courses, visits and exchanges, defence trade, collaboration, co-production, and research and development in defence.

Operative Hindrances

A survey of the nature of hindrances that arose is necessary to gauge their impact and thereafter suggest remedial measures. The first issue is adverse political conditions. In 1992, succumbing to the American pressure, Russia refused to transfer critical cryogenic engine technology to India. This posed a significant constraint for the development of the Indian space programme. Glavkosmos, as part of the deal with Indian Space Research Organisation (ISRO), was required to make available the cryogenic engine technology. But its refusal to supply the technology led to a deterioration in the same relationship between the two countries.[9] India also went through a certain period of political uncertainties, particularly between 1996 and 1999 when there was political instability with governments lasting for short periods.

The situation, thereafter, has been considerably stable. In Russia in the post-Putin period, Indo-Russian relations have become a matter of national consensus, thereby providing continuity. President Medvedev has followed up on policies laid down previously as indicated during his visit to India in December 2008, for the annual dialogue. He has shown a desire to raise the relationship to a higher trajectory in the years ahead.[10] This is a positive indicator for the future.

Turning to other issues, at the operative level, the absence of an intellectual property right (IPR) agreement has become a "tangible barrier" to the joint development of sophisticated weapons and cutting-edge defence technologies between India and Russia.[11] There are constraints, as Russian laws may not permit the transfer of technologies without such an agreement. Negotiations are on, but this would be an important factor to dissuade joint development particularly with two important projects, fifth generation fighter aircraft and transport aircraft in the pipeline.

Similarly, the Integrity Pact is an issue with India.[12] After promulgation of the Defence Procurement Procedure (DPP) 2006, duly amended in 2008, every defence contract by India requires that the foreign vendor has to sign an integrity pact which denotes that there is no commission or any other type of incentive provided by either party where the contract amount exceeds Rs. 100 crore. India's past experience, when there was corruption by middlemen in the 155 mm Bofors gun deal, has led to the inclusion of this clause in the DPP. Russia, on the other hand, has concentrated defence exports under a single corporation which facilitates trade and negotiations. However, this is not a manufacturer but a trading firm, hence it may be unable to enter into such an agreement. Thus, legal and other complications between Rosoboronexport on one hand, the original Russian manufacturer on the other, and the requirement of the Integrity Pact by India, may be one of the problems.

Russia has told the Indian Ministry of Defence that some clauses of the Integrity Pact "collide with" the domestic laws of the country. Russian reservations have got to do with the pact, demanding an explicit commitment against payment of commissions and appointment of agents.[13] To an extent the problem is restricted so far, since the purchase of 40 Sukhoi, 30 fighters and more than 300 T-90 tanks are "repeat orders", where Integrity Pact does not come into play. However, in all future deals, this could be a major hindrance for Russia to win contracts in India.

A critical issue which is emerging is that of quality control due to major problems that have come up with regard to technology transfer.[14] The indigenous manufacture of 1000 T-90S battle tanks, with critical technological elements by the Heavy Vehicles Factory at Avadi near Chennai, has been impacted due to this constraint. India has also withheld payment for one of the three IL-38 maritime patrol aircraft, upgraded with the Sea Dragon submarine detection equipment, due to its poor quality. Similarly, it has refused to take delivery of the Kilo class submarine and land attack missiles as during trials there was sub-optimal performance of the missiles which failed to hit the target a number of times.[15] Delays in the provision of spares and ancillary support are a related problem, as was in the past.[16]

Another key area of concern emerging is the transfer of the nuclear powered Akula class submarine as reported in the media, though no official confirmation is obviously available regarding this deal. It is believed that India and Russia have drawn up a five-year, $350 million deal to lease two Akula-II class nuclear-powered attack submarines. The Akula class is to be an important step in the Indian acquisition of a second strike capability based under water; it is a silent, nuclear-powered submarine which is able to dive up to 600 metres and achieve submerged speed of 33 knots. This submarine was to be a follow-up to INS Chakra, the Charlie class submarine operated by the Indian Navy from 1988–1991, and was to make up for the gap till India's indigenous nuclear powered submarine. Advanced Technology Vessel (ATV) was commissioned some time in the early part of the next decade.[17]

The Russian Nerpa submarine was to provide Indian sailors valuable experience, before they operated the indigenous nuclear powered submarine. However, on 8 November 2008, it was reported that the fire extinguishing system aboard the Nerpa, the nuclear powered attack submarine, inadvertently-triggered, resulting in an accident which caused 20 deaths. The gas was contained after hatches dividing the vessel's compartments sealed themselves automatically.[18] This has caused renewed concerns about Russian technology in a highly sensitive area. It can be seen that to some extent, Russia's military revival and its reputation as a credible purveyor of armaments to foreign powers has suffered in the past. Hopefully, things will improve with greater investment.

Another critical issue which is now creating concerns is that of pricing.[19] From May 2007, Russia has sought increase in the price for all defence deals including those already signed. The $8.5 billion Sukhoi deal with 40 aircraft at the current cost escalation rate of 2.55 per cent per annum was the first in focus.[20] Similarly, the price of the aircraft carrier Gorshkov has also come up for repeated discussion. An additional payment of $1.2 billion for retrofitting and modernisation of the Admiral Gorshkov, a 44,750 tonne Kiev class aircraft carrier, has been sought whereas the original cost was said to be $1.5 billion.[21] It is said that Russian shipbuilders had not envisaged the extent of refurbishment required, thereby leading to the present situation. What is worrying for India, is that the aircraft carrier which was due to be supplied by 2008-09 is now likely to reach the country only by 2012-2013, that too if there is an early agreement on the price. This has left a critical gap in India's defence capability as presently the country has no aircraft carrier at sea. The INS Viraat is also under refurbishment in Mumbai and is only due out in 2010. The Gorshkov, to be renamed as INS Vikramaditya, is to cover this gap.

The issue of debt clearance with the collapse of the Soviet Union, fluctuations in currencies over the years, and exchange rates swinging from one end to another has also been a cause of concern. As an Indian official remarked, "Goodwill alone cannot forge mutually advantageous economic ties. Trade between Russia and India almost collapsed in 1991-1992 because of arguments over the rupee-rouble exchange rate and the amount India owed Russia as the successor state to the USSR."[22] India had an amassed debt of $12-16 billion, owed to the Soviet Union for arms purchases.[23] Disputes varied from nature of the currency, and exchange rate that would be used. With Russia facing an economically critical situation during this period, debt clearance became a financial tool rather than a strategic balancer in the relationship. Now that both countries have stable economies despite the global financial crunch, it is expected that there would be parity in affiliation in the years ahead.

Overcoming Hindrances

Having surveyed the hindrances, it would be evident that given the nature of current relations between the two countries with firm leadership provided by President Dmitry Medvedev and stability in governance under Prime Minister Vladimir Putin, there is much scope for improvement in Indo-Russian defence relations.

The overall aim of enhancing defence cooperation would be to utilise the potential for strategic engagement in other fields between both the countries, presently restricted to the field of defence acquisitions. The scope for this is manifold and could range from training to security dialogue and exercises. For instance, Russia's nuclear, biological and chemical (NBC) defence experience and capabilities can be positively useful for the Indian armed forces. Another area is the operation of nuclear powered submarines. These are fields of strategic significance for India wherein building competencies would require assistance from countries with an experience bank in this sphere. Having identified India's relationship with Russia as a strategic one, there is scope for engagement in this sphere.

Other areas include training for officers in courses and exchange of high level delegations, aerospace exploration, maritime cooperation in the Indian Ocean and Special Forces exercises, and sharing of experience in cold weather warfare. The Indian armed forces have much to offer in terms of experience in counter-terrorism which can be of mutual benefit. Streamlining acquisitions is another area to overcome periodic problems which have been recurring over the years. There is also enough scope for joint projects in defence research and development, and special projects on the lines of the BrahMos. Some suggestions may therefore be in order.

At the apex level, a key issue for consideration is inclusion of inter services dialogue.[24] While at present, there is a strategic security dialogue between the Ministries of Defence, this has not been followed up down to the services. While the Indo-Russian dialogue has matured at the political level, closer interaction between the services would improve understanding, and develop greater cooperation based on mutual considerations. This dialogue can extend to a number of current issues as international terrorism, non-proliferation of weapons of mass destruction and timely delivery of assistance and rehabilitation during and after major natural disasters. Developing in depth relationship is, thus, envisaged to generate an overall momentum.

Another institutional issue is that of empowering commissions. There are a number of commissions between Indian and Russian defence authorities. The Governmental Commission on Military-Technical Cooperation (IRIGC-MTC) deals with a number of issues such as supply of defence systems, equipment upgrade, product and life cycle support for defence equipment of Russian origin.[25] It also covers issues like licensed and joint production, joint development and production of systems and platforms, interaction between the two armed forces and military-technical cooperation. While this Commission is constituted at the level of secretaries, it is not seen to be fully empowered to facilitate speedy decision-making. Moreover, different sub-groups and working groups need to meet to resolve issues and provide inputs to the Commission to take final decisions. Empowering the IRIGC–MTC and the sub-groups is recommended, so that decisions are taken more speedily and momentum is generated at the operative level.

The inhibitions on intellectual property rights and Integrity Pact between the two countries need to be removed. India has recently adopted a model for transfer of technology from France for the Scorpene, which can act as a guideline. Russia would have to resolve the internal legal issues that arise from its military industrial organisation centring around Rosoboronexport, which is inhibiting it from signing the Integrity Pact with India.[26]

Joint development of arms, aircraft, missiles and military equipment is an area which will also provide the much needed boost to defence cooperation between the two countries. An ideal example is that of BrahMos. This has moved beyond the technology demonstration stage and has been operationalised by the Indian Army and the Navy. Taking the same forward to BrahMos II, which in India is called as the Brahmastra (all-powerful weapon), would be another step in enhancing cooperation. BrahMos II will be a hypersonic missile which will evade detection, deliver lethal pay load and prevent response by hostile air defence weapons.

As the former President Dr. A.P.J. Abdul Kalam said some time back, "In the emerging network centric warfare scenario, fast deployment of hypersonic missile systems will be necessary to maintain our force level supremacy. I visualize long range hypersonic cruise missiles not only delivering pay loads but also returning to the base after the mission, leading to re-usable class of cruise missiles within the next decade."[27] The characteristics of such a missile are envisaged to hypersonic speed between 4 to 6 Mach, range upwards of 1000 kms, altitudes 20,000 to 30,000 metres with a warhead weighing over 300 kgs. This would be a lethal armament which can cause heavy destruction and casualties at the terminal end.[28] Similarly, joint projects as the joint development and production of multi-role transport aircraft and fifth generation fighter aircraft should be undertaken speedily with allotment of fiscal and technical resources. Russian support will be needed to overcome the bane of slow progress in project management by the DRDO.

Another field where there can be greater cooperation is that of training exercises. Russia has a wealth of experience in this field. The joint anti-terror exercise involving Russia, India and China along with some other member states of the Shanghai Cooperation Organisation (SCO) like Uzbekistan, Kazakhstan, Tajikistan or Kyrgyzstan are taking place on a regular basis. If organisational constraints do not permit such a venture, exercises can be held bilaterally, thereby enhancing the skills of the Indian armed forces which have considerable experience in a number of areas such as counter-terrorism and insurgency, high altitude and cold weather warfare and so on.

Similarly, yearly exercises such as the Indra series at sea should be increased in terms of participation. In the year 2008, the exercise was at a reduced scale with only one ship, Peter the Great, participating from the Russian side.[29] With Gulf of Aden encountering piracy, joint maritime exercises between the two countries will go a long way in enhancing security, apart from providing training benefits to both sides. Similarly, Special Forces exercises and joint training is another area where there is a scope for sharing expertise.

With modification of the Indian defence procurement procedure, Indian defence acquisitions are likely to be open to many competitors. Given Russia's deep understanding of India's defence requirements, Moscow will continue to have an edge over others. However, Russian companies would have to expect more competition, and therefore be ready to follow norms laid down in the procurement process. At the same time, India cannot rely on "friendship prices" from Russia and has to be prepared to buy at market prices. Indian authorities need to consider that the question is not just about pricing but also of maintaining a strategic edge; for many of the platforms provided by Russia will be the mainstay of the defence forces of the country for decades to come.

Maintenance support is another field where India will be looking towards Russia in the years ahead. This is particularly so with the possible acquisition of nuclear submarines, which will complicate maintenance and logistics with a highly diverse force of submarines sourced from Germany, Russia and now the Scorpene from France. Russian experience in servicing the submarine fleet can come in handy for Indian dockyards and reduce the need for moving these to Russian ports for this purpose.

Russia overcame the slump in its defence industry in the 1990s when only 20 per cent or so was functional. For the period 2000-2004, Moscow regained its pre-eminence in the field of production and export of conventional weapons.[30] This is evidently an outcome of the progressive measures undertaken by Russian leadership which are likely to continue. Thus, there are unlikely to be any breakdowns in defence supplies from Russia in the future, which has been one of India's greatest worries in the past two decades or so, since the collapse of the Soviet Union. Now these are issues of the past.

Developing a Strategic Partnership

India and Russia need to look beyond the periodic crisis, economic and political, to weave a strategic partnership which at present appears to be more in terms of a concept than implemented on the ground. Some of the areas have already been highlighted but their strategic impact needs some consideration. One such issue is that of acquisition of a nuclear powered submarine by India.

The Indian navy's blue water ambitions extend from the Persian Gulf to the Malacca Straits. In the south, the entire expanse of the Indian Ocean is sought to be covered. Indian stations in Antarctica and the Exclusive Economic Zone (EEZ) also form a part of the area of naval influence. This is a very large area. Thus, for India, acquisition of an aircraft carrier and a set of nuclear submarines is important. The submarine of Akula class has considerable advantages, being nuclear powered; it is necessary for a blue water navy, if it is to cover a vast maritime sphere off the continental shelf.

India's peninsular configuration astride the Indian Ocean, necessitates deployment of a considerable quantum of blue water assets with an ability to foray far and wide for sustained periods. A nuclear submarine provides just such a capability. Another advantage of the Akula, is the low acoustic signature of the submarine which will be a considerable tactical advantage.

Nuclear submarines are considered as essential strategic assets and vital components of a credible second strike capability. This will be the key component of India's nuclear deterrence once fully armed with nuclear tipped Submarine Launched Ballistic Missiles (SLBMs) or Submarine Launched Cruise Missiles (SLCMs), both categories under development (Sagarika and BrahMos). Given the limited range of these missiles, Akula class with a low acoustic signature can probably approach the area of interest much more easily. The need to keep this deterrence at sea for long periods also necessitates a nuclear rather than a conventional submarine, as the former has extended endurance. The other objective of acquisition of a nuclear submarine is to enhance the reach and endurance of the Indian navy, now increasingly striving to extend influence over a wider area. Any strategic inhibitions would be unfounded, for the main objective for acquisition of Akula class is essentially to create expertise in operation of nuclear submarines till the Indian Advanced Technology Vessel (ATV) project bears fruit.

The Akula class will reduce time for training and adaptation of personnel from conventional to nuclear submarining on induction of ATV. This will also considerably assist in developing processes and procedures for nuclear submarine operations which is a very intricate and hazardous assignment. Thus, essentially, Akula class is an interim phase of submarine development for the Indian navy's nuclear programme which will make up the gap till ATV is inducted. Eventually, India is planning to have five nuclear submarines. For such a large fleet, development of operational expertise is essential but time consuming. The Akula will considerably reduce the time of integration.

The Indian navy has had experience of operating the INS Chakra which was on lease from the Soviet navy, but was returned in 1991. The Soviets did not provide access to the reactor of INS Chakra which continued to be manned by Russian personnel.[31] The arrangements that will be worked out for the Akula are not clear. However, given the symmetry in relationship *vis-a-vis* the early 1990s, there is all probability that an Indian crew will be controlling the reactor of Akula class as and when leased. This will further reduce the deployment timings for ATV. As it is also believed, that the hull and reactor design of the ATV is based on the new Russian Project 885 Severodvinsk Class and 190 MW pressurised water reactor as per Federation of American Scientists, Indian submariners would gain valuable experience in this field.[32]

Projects as the Akula will, thus, be a test case for the development of the Indo-Russian defence partnership in the years ahead. It is such projects that both nations should look at, to foster a better military military relationship.

Conclusion

Military cooperation is a major component of New Delhi's strategic relationship with Moscow. However, it needs to be expanded to fields other than equipment acquisitions, suggestions for which have been included in this chapter. While all areas may not show promise from the very outset, a beginning can be made to look beyond the MiGs and T-90s to diversify interaction in the years ahead.

This cooperation provides mutual benefits to both sides. India has been dependent on the best platforms provided by Russia, be it tanks, ships, submarines, fighters or transport aircrafts at friendship or favourable prices. Russian equipment has, thus, been a backbone of the Indian military over the past many decades. On the other hand, 800 Russian defence production facilities were kept in operation by Indian defence contracts at a critical time when Moscow was undergoing a heavy financial and political crunch. Russian exports to China and India amount to 41 per cent of the total revenue brought in by Russia's defence industry.

The strategic partnership between both the countries is, therefore, a long lasting relationship with mutual benefits; it has a long future ahead despite the episodic hindrances. The need of the day is to continue to diversify the same, which is currently biased towards arms and equipment supply and manufacturing to other areas as joint training and exercises, maritime integration and related fields.

End Notes

1. Ministry of Defence. *Annual Report 2003-04*. Government of India. Available at *www.mod.nic.in*
2. Muthanna, K.A. (2006). "Enabling military to military cooperation as foreign policy tool: Options for India", *Knowledge World*. New Delhi, p 3.
3. Ibid.: 21-22.
4. Hui, Wang and Du Wenjuan (2009). "Chinese naval fleet sails into Gulf of Aden", *China Daily*, 06 January. Available at *http://www.chinadaily.com.cn/china/2009-01/06/content_7371034.htm*
5. Patankar, Vinayak (2007). "Importance of Indo-Russian military-technical cooperation and future prospects", *ORF Discourse* 2(9), December. New Delhi: Observer Research Foundation.
6. Ibid.
7. Conley, Jerome M. (2006). "Indo Russian military and nuclear cooperation: Implications for US security interests", INSS *Occasional Paper* 31. *Proliferation Series*. February. Available at *http://www.fas.org/nuke/guide/india/doctrine/ocp31.htm*
8. Ibid.
9. Ibid.

10. Embassy of India Moscow (2008). "President Dmitry Medvedev visits India", December 5. Available at *http://indianembassy.ru/cms/index.php?option=com_content&task=view&id=570&Itemid=625*

11. Bakshi, Jyotsna (2006). "India-Russia defence co-operation", *Strategic Analysis* 30(2): 475, April-June.

12. Ministry of Defence. "India and Russia sign a landmark agreement for joint development and production of fifth generation fighter aircraft", Govt. of India. Available at *http://pib.nic.in/release/rel_print_page.asp?relid=32016*

13. *Financial Express* (2006). "Indo-Russian defence deals yet to be sorted out", 20 June. Available at *http://www.financialexpress.com/news/indorussian-defence-deals-yet-to-be-sorted-out/202012/0*

14. Bakshi, Jyotsna. *op.cit.*: 456.

15. Press Trust of India Report, "India refuses upgraded submarines from Russia". Available at *http://ibnlive.in.com/news/india-refuses-upgraded-submarines-from-russia/56293-3.html*, DoA.

16. Bakshi, Jyotsna. *op.cit.*: 453.

17. There are a number of sources which indicate lease of Akula class submarines from Russia to India. Only some of these have been cited. A report in the *India Today*, "The secret nuke sub deal", by Sandeep Unnithan in the 3 September 2007 issue available at *http://indiatoday.intoday.in/index.php?option=com_ content&Itemid=1&task=view&id=1024&sectionid=40&issueid=15&latn=2* or Domain B, "India expecting to take delivery of Russian Akula II nuclear powered submarine next year" may be relevant and is available at *http://www.domain-b.com/defence/general/20080703_akula.html*. Jyotsna Bakshi, Note 11 also speaks of the Akula deal

18. *Ria Novosti*. "What happened on the Nerpa?" Available at *http://en.rian.ru/analysis/20081110/118224041.html*

19. Bakshi, Jyotsna. *op.cit.*: 455.

20. *Financial Express (2006)*. Note 13. In addition, there are a number of reports in the Indian and Russian media on the price escalation issue.

21. Prasad, K.V. (2009). "Team to hold talks on Gorshkov price", *The Hindu Report*, 27 January. Available at *http://www.hindu.com/2009/01/27/stories/2009012759521300.htm*.

22. Conley, Jerome M. *op.cit.*

23. Ibid.

24. Patankar, Vinayak. *op.cit.*

25. Ministry of Defence (India), Note 12.

26. Patankar, Vinayak. *op.cit.*

27. Embassy of the Russian Federation in the Republic of India. Address of the President of India, H.E. Dr. A.P.J. Abdul Kalam, during the Commencement of delivery of BrahMos missile systems to the Indian Army (New Delhi, 21 June, 2007). Available at *http://www.rusembassy.in/eng/?menu=ambassador/sp_menu&page=ambassador/2007_3*

28. Nagra, R.S. (2006). "Brahmastra of future wars", *Air Power Journal* 3(1): 31, Spring (January-March).

29. Dutta, Sujan (2009). "Play, not game, for Peter the Great - Russian sailors 'recuperate' on Goa beach after exercise is downscaled", *The Daily Telegraph*, 31 January. Available at *http://www.telegraphindia.com/1090131/jsp/frontpage/story_10465832.jsp*
30. Bakshi, Jyotsna. *op.cit.*: 462.
31. Conley, Jerome M. *op.cit.* and sources as quoted at Note 17.
32. Ibid.

4 India-Russia Energy Cooperation

Devika Sharma

No country other than Russia has been so intimately woven with India and its history. Despite the historical legacy, however, the India-Russia friendship was one of the casualties of the post-Cold War era. Along with the disintegration of the Soviet Union, came a nadir in India's relationship with Russia. Today, that relationship remains in a state of flux—far from the sound footing it stood upon before the Cold War ended. As the two countries try to regain its lost momentum, energy can be seen as an increasingly important constituent of the India-Russia partnership in the future. It is this dimension of the partnership between the two countries that this chapter seeks to assess and highlight.

Unlike in the past, where political ideology and international power configurations brought India and Russia close to each other, today the impetus for greater engagement lies in simple demand and supply complementarities. What are these complementarities in the energy sector specifically? How are the energy sector complementarities impacting the India-Russia partnership and how can this dimension of the partnership be expanded? What are the obstacles that need to be addressed before energy can be seen as playing a larger role in the India-Russia partnership? It is some of these important questions that this chapter will seek to address.

The Energy Synergy between India and Russia

The important role energy can play in solidifying the India-Russia partnership rests on a simple fact—that of demand-supply complementarities between India and Russia. On the demand side, India offers Russia a growing economy with a rising demand for energy. With dwindling reserves and little prospect of finding new reserves to meet rising demand, import dependency is projected to increase for India across all major fuel types. Before the current financial crisis, the Integrated Energy Policy projected that India's import dependency for commercial energy for the year 2031-32, in order to maintain an 8 per cent GDP growth rate, would rise between 90-93 per cent for oil, 0-49 per cent for natural gas and 11-45 per cent for coal (Planning Commission, 2006).

According to the International Energy Agency (IEA), India's projected demand for the main fuels such as oil, coal, natural gas and nuclear can be seen in Figure 4.1 below.

Figure 4.1

India's Rising Demand for Energy (Million Tonne of Oil Equivalent)

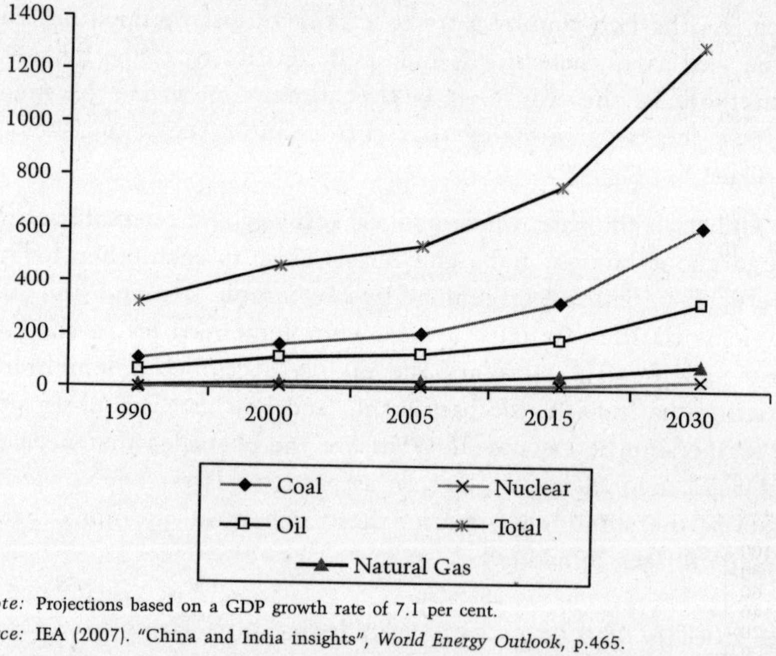

Note: Projections based on a GDP growth rate of 7.1 per cent.
Source: IEA (2007). "China and India insights", *World Energy Outlook*, p.465.

India's import dependency is also set to rise. In business as usual scenario, a study carried out by TERI projects the import dependency across major fuel types (coal, oil and natural gas) and can be seen from Figure 4.2 (PSA Report 2006).

Figure 4.2

A. Coal Production and Import Dependency

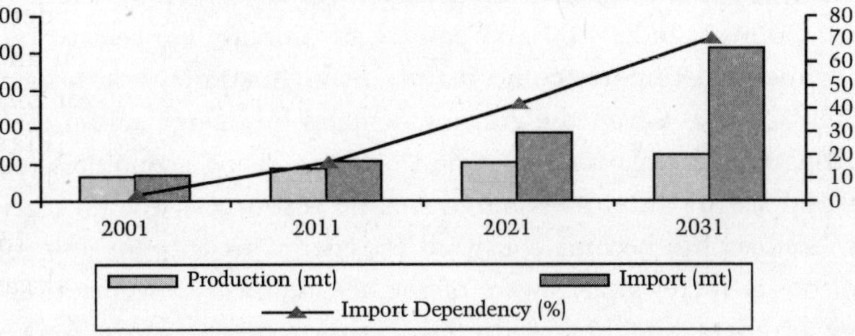

B. Oil Production and Import Dependency

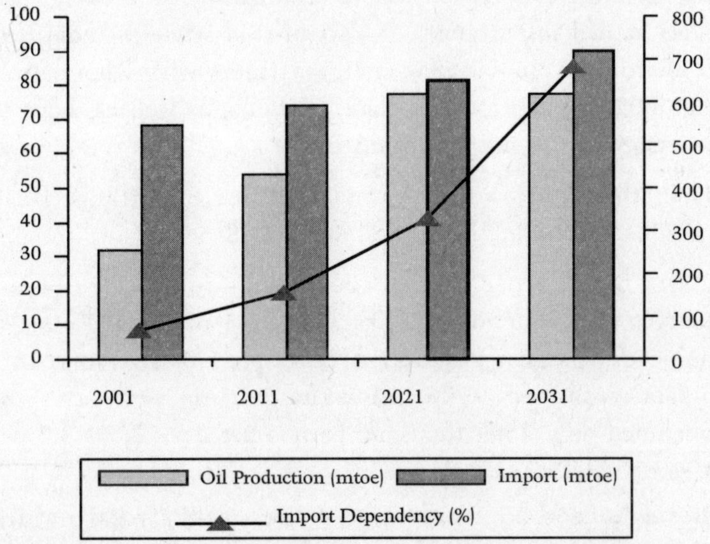

C. Natural Gas Production and Import Dependency

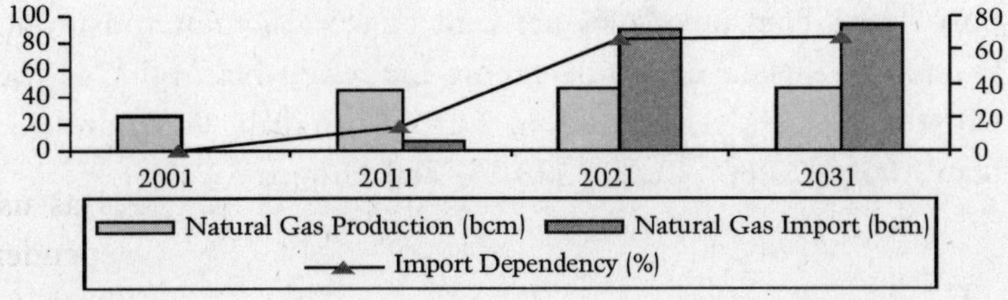

Source: TERI, 2006.

The figures show the broad reality of India's growing energy demand and dependency. Energy security for India, therefore, depends on assured and secure supplies of energy to meet future demand. At the present moment, India's oil and natural gas imports are centred on West Asia, while coal imports come mainly from Australia, South-East Asia and South Africa. Given the growing demand for energy across the world as well as the attendant competition between rising economies (such as India and China) for increasingly scarce resources, diversification of energy sources has become a byword for energy security for any country. India, too, is increasingly aware of the geographical concentration of its energy imports and how vulnerable this concentration makes the country to any possible instability or conflict that might flare up in West Asia. It is for this reason that diversification as a energy securing strategy has gained importance. As part of this strategy, India has been trying to identify favourable new energy partners with whom, India can enhance its bilateral political and trade relations, as well as, hope to gain access to energy in the not so distant future.

It is in this context that Russia assumes importance in India's energy calculus. According to BP Statistics 2008:

- Russia has 6.4 per cent of the world's total oil reserves with reserves to production (R/P) ratio of 21.8 per cent. Russia is also the second largest producer of oil after Saudi Arabia. In 2007, Russia produced 9978 thousand barrels per day, while it consumed only 2699 thousand barrels per day (about 3.2 per cent of world total).
- Russia houses 25.2 per cent of the world's total natural gas reserves and has a R/P ratio of 37.5 per cent. In 2007, Russia produced 607.4 billion cubic metres (bcm), while it consumed only 438.8 bcm (about 15 per cent of world's total consumption). Presently, Russia does not export Liquefied Natural Gas (LNG). Most of Russia's gas goes to Europe (mainly Germany (35.55 bcm); Italy (23.80), Turkey (23.15) and Hungary (7.85)).

Figure 4.3

Russia's Consumption versus Reserves as Percentage of Total

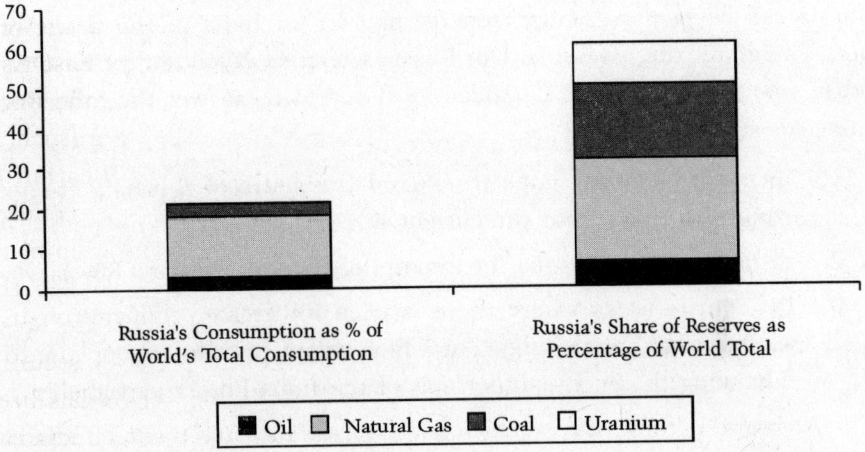

Source: *BP Statistics 2008* and World Nuclear Association.

- Russia has 18.5 per cent share of the world's total coal reserves, and has an R/P ratio of 500. In 2007, Russia produced 148.2 mtoe of coal and consumed 94.5 mtoe (about 3.0 per cent of world's total coal consumption).
- Russia is also a rich source of uranium—the third largest in the world. It has 10 per cent of the world's uranium reserves (after Australia—with 23 per cent and Kazakhstan with 15 per cent), according to the World Nuclear Association.[1]

Given these basic complementarities, on both the demand and supply side, energy can indeed be seen as a critical arena for cooperation between India and Russia. However, these basic demand-supply synergies do not grasp the obstacles that stand in the way of enhancing the energy dimension of the partnership between the two countries. The following section therefore brings to light some of the key obstacles, concerns and issues that together help "assess" Russia's favourability as an energy partner for India.

Assessing Russia

Even though India is already importing some amounts of coal and oil from Russia, India's diversification strategy needs to pin down whether Russia can be seen as a bigger energy partner for India in the future or not. Therefore, the assessment of Russia's relative favourability *vis-à-vis* other new energy partners is guided by the need to answer the following three questions:

1. To see if there is scope to expand the share of Russia's energy exports to India from the current levels.
2. To look at the potential for imports of natural gas from Russia.
3. To identify areas where there is need for greater cooperation in sectors other than energy, but which might provide an impetus to enhancing the energy dimension of the India-Russia partnership.

Answers to these three questions, requires an assessment of Russia on the basis of a broad range of parameters. The parameters together facilitate in identifying the obstacles that stand in the way of Russia assuming a larger role in India's energy sector; the risks that a consuming country like India might have to incur by looking at Russia in a bigger way; the larger geopolitical compulsions that are necessary to take into consideration while deepening India's energy cooperation; the scope for improving India's bilateral political and trade relations; and the energy sector-specific factors and infrastructural concerns that will ultimately determine the form and substance of the energy cooperation.

The parameters can therefore be divided into the following five broad categories:

- Energy sector concerns.
- India-specific indicators.
- Geopolitical alignments/concerns.
- Secure routes.
- Risk ratings.

Energy Sector-Specific Parameters

Apart from available exportable surplus and the promise of future discoveries, it is also important to assess India's relative importance *vis-*

à-vis Russia's key energy importers. This is not the least important because an assessment of Russia's favourability as a potential energy exporter to India, depends to a great extent on where India finds itself in Russia's choice of countries as key energy importers.

Therefore, it must be stated at the outset that Russia's other key energy partners are in Europe. As a result, Russia's energy security and related foreign policy concerns are centred in Europe. Russia's oil exports, in the form of fuel oil or diesel oil, for example, are mainly bound for Western Europe—for countries such as Germany, Belarus, Ukraine, Poland, Hungary, Slovakia and the Czech Republic. Most of Russia's natural gas goes to Europe too—mainly Germany (35.55 bcm); Italy (23.80), Turkey (23.15) and Hungary (7.85). The exportable surplus of coal has been minor and Russia has been focusing on expanding its domestic consumption of coal in order to free up natural gas for export. This, among other factors, was responsible for Russia's plummeting coal exports in the year 2008; a trend which is likely to continue until 2009-2010. Russia's domestic demand for coal is set to rise from the current 130 million tonnes a year to about 326 million tonnes (*Reuters*, 2007a). Therefore, the fall in coal exports will continue in the coming years. This is what India will need to keep in mind even as Russian exporters seek out India as a new steam coal market, and India itself struggles to locate high quality steam coal (see *Reuters*, 2007b).

Apart from Europe, Russia is also increasingly expanding its energy exports to the East, given the fact that it is flanked on one side by two of the most energy-hungry economies, that is, China and India. Thus far, however, Russia's eyes have been mostly set on China and Japan, and the country's eastward gaze is centred on the Eastern Siberian Pacific Ocean pipeline. The pipeline will pipe oil from Taishet in Eastern Siberia via Skovorodino and onto Kozmino Bay, southeast of Nakhodka. Both Japan and China have been bargaining hard to acquire access to this East Siberian oil. However, the negotiations and cost differentials have left the ultimate direction of the pipeline in ambivalence. A spur from the Eastern Siberian pipeline can extend southwards from Skovorodino to Daqing in China and reach the Chinese market. While this would be the far cheaper option for Russia, the other option to extend the pipeline to Kozmino Bay would make it possible for Russian oil to reach other Asian and North American consumers across the Pacific Ocean. The eventual route of the map would also impact possible oil exports to India—an outlet on the Pacific Ocean could also be accessed by India, along with other importers in Asia and North America. However, despite the ambivalence over the route of this pipeline, the fact that needs to be underscored is that Asia is an increasingly important region for Russia and its energy exports. According to Russia's Energy Strategy for 2001-2030, Russia hopes to expand its total export of oil to the Asia Pacific region and Southern Asia from 7 per cent today to about 30 per cent and about 25 per cent for natural gas from the current levels of 5 per cent (See Legvold, 2008).

Apart from Russia's key energy partners, the other factor that needs to be taken into consideration while assessing Russia's favourability is the energy sector concerns prevailing within the country. The promise of Russian oil reaching its projected destination and meeting proposed targets will ultimately depend on factors such as domestic demand and the energy sector challenges that Russia faces. Demand in Russia is undoubtedly rising—as has been mentioned above; domestic demand for coal has already begun to impact exports. Similarly, ageing capital stock requires greater investments. Russia also requires greater investments in the oil refining sector; according to Mr. Oganesyan, head of the Federal Energy Agency (Rosenergo), the investments in Russia's oil refining sector must run into 131 billion roubles by 2010 (*RusEnergy,* 2005). While there is great promise of undiscovered oil reserves—possibly as much as 77 billion barrels of oil a day, the fact is that currently, Russia's known reserves are fast depleting. Therefore, Russia and other energy consuming countries interested in Russia will need to push for exploration in a bigger way in the coming decades.

Infrastructure concerns for export are also equally important. Russia has in recent years faced reduced export capacity, particularly pipelines. Rail accounts for 5 per cent of Russia's crude oil exports, and this will increase if Russia does not expand its pipeline capacity in the coming decades. However, for exports to Asia, until the East Siberian Pacific Ocean pipeline comes online, rail exports to countries such as China will remain the preferred mode of transportation. At present, Russian crude oil is exported via rail to the northeast cities of Harbin and Daqing and to Central China via Mongolia. Rail exports of crude oil to China increased from approximately 200,000 bbl/d in 2005 to 300,000 bbl/d by 2006 according to China's Ministry of Railways (Energy Information Analysis, 2008: 8).

Russian oil as a possible fillip for India's import, needs to take into consideration the interplay between global oil prices and its impact on Russia's economy. Falling oil prices in recent months, for instance, have impacted Russia's economy negatively. The revenue of the government is dependent on oil prices, set at a certain level. That is, Russia's 2008 budget is based on oil prices of US$ 92 per barrel. The country witnessed several protests in almost every major city as a result of the downturn in the global economy, and the fact that the Russian economy has not been able to ride the wave of rising oil prices, as it could during the earlier part of 2008. With falling oil prices, Russia has also shown greater interest in joining the Organization of the Petroleum Exporting Countries (OPEC), and according to *The Economist*, is "inadvertently supporting OPEC efforts to stabilise the oil price" (*The Economist*, 2008). Although Russia has had observer status at OPEC since 1998, the current downturn in the global economy and the falling oil prices might, in the not-so-distant future, push Russia to join its ranks. Although many claim this unlikely, pointing to the advantages Russia has in "free-riding", India needs to build this into a possible future scenario, given the fact that India has already been pushing for a greater dialogue between producer and consumer countries in the world.

India-Specific Indicators

As mentioned above, India's relations with Russia have faced both ups and downs. As a country with which India seeks to expand its energy cooperation, Russia is more than a suitable choice, given the historical linkages and the established patterns of cooperation in a wide range of sectors.

To begin with, any future cooperation between India and Russia in the energy sector does not have to pave the way afresh. Instead, there is already considerable engagement between the two countries in several arenas. Most importantly, India and Russia share a high level strategic partnership since 2000, when the two countries signed the Strategic

Partnership to take their relations to a higher level. Apart from high-level visits, India and Russia also have a long-standing cooperation in the defence sector. Although it has been a sore point in recent years, the fact of the matter is that, there continues to be a broad engagement in this sector. According to Stockholm International Peace Research Institute (SIPRI) Yearbook 2008, Russia exports about 22 per cent of its total supplies to India (and about 45 per cent of it goes to China).

More importantly, India and Russia have already been cooperating in the energy sector. In the atomic energy sector, for instance, Russia has been India's key partner for decades. At present, Russia is helping India build two nuclear units with 1,000 MW light water reactors at Koodankulam. Talks have been at an advanced stage, for further collaboration on four additional units at Koodankulam. Russia has also offered India the option of investing in its upcoming uranium enrichment centre at Angarsk, Siberia, in lieu of paying for nuclear fuel to be supplied to the Koodankulam nuclear station, which is being built with Russian assistance (Sasi, 2008). Earlier in 2009, Russia's leading nuclear company TVEL and India's Department of Atomic Energy (DAE), signed contracts for supplying 2000 tonnes of natural uranium pellets for India's pressurised heavy water reactors and another contract for 60 tonne low enriched uranium (LEU) pellets for boiling water reactor units at Tarapur, Maharashtra (Sinha, 2009). Other examples of cooperation in the energy sector between Russia and India include the following:

- ONGC Videsh Limited (OVL) has a 20 per cent stake in Sakhalin-I and has invested about US$ 1.7 billion in the project;
- In 2008, Russia offered the possibility of a joint venture in Sakhalin-III between OVL and Rosneft;
- Russian firms are keen on participating in the latest round of auction of oil and gas blocks under New Exploration Licensing Policy (NELP); cooperation in hydroelectric and thermal power sectors has been suggested; development of new oil and gas fields;
- Rosneft is interested in ONGC's proposed LNG terminal in Mangalore;

- Gazprom and Gas Authority of India Limited (GAIL) have jointly developed a gas block in the Bay of Bengal.

While there has been considerable engagement at the strategic level and the energy sector, there is much that can be achieved in the trade and investment sector. Currently, India's energy trade with Russia is minimal. The share of Russia's imports, in India's total imports (of goods) is a meagre 0.98 per cent, amounting in 2007-08 to US$ 2468.49 million (EXIM Bank). India's share in Russia's total imports from the world is similarly meagre, a little over 1 per cent of Russia's total external trade volume. Surprisingly, this fell from the 1.2 per cent share that India held in 1997 (MoCI). Of this total trade, India's energy imports from Russia constitute only about 6 per cent of total imports of goods from Russia, as Figure 4.4 shows.

While the level of bilateral trade and investment between India and Russia leaves much to be desired, India and Russia have started to make an honest attempt at intensifying their trade relations. As part of the initiative to enhance their relations, 2009 was declared the Year of India in Russia.

Geopolitical Alignments and Concerns

When assessing a country, apart from the availability of exportable surplus and good bilateral relations, it is also necessary to take into consideration the larger geopolitical alignments. Geopolitical concerns could go a long way in constraining or influencing the degree of "favourability" that both Russia and India accord each other. That is, commitments to other key partners or alliances would in a great way influence the foreign policy choices and power configurations for both Russia and India.

At the outset, Russia's relations with the West—particularly the United States and its erstwhile satellites in Eastern Europe, are not particularly stable. At international foras, Russia continues to stress upon the need to move towards multipolarity in the international system, and perceives the manoeuverings by the US in its immediate neighbourhood as a threat to its sovereignty. In the light of the recently concluded India-US civil nuclear deal, India must keep in mind Russia's

Figure 4.4

India's Energy Imports from Russia

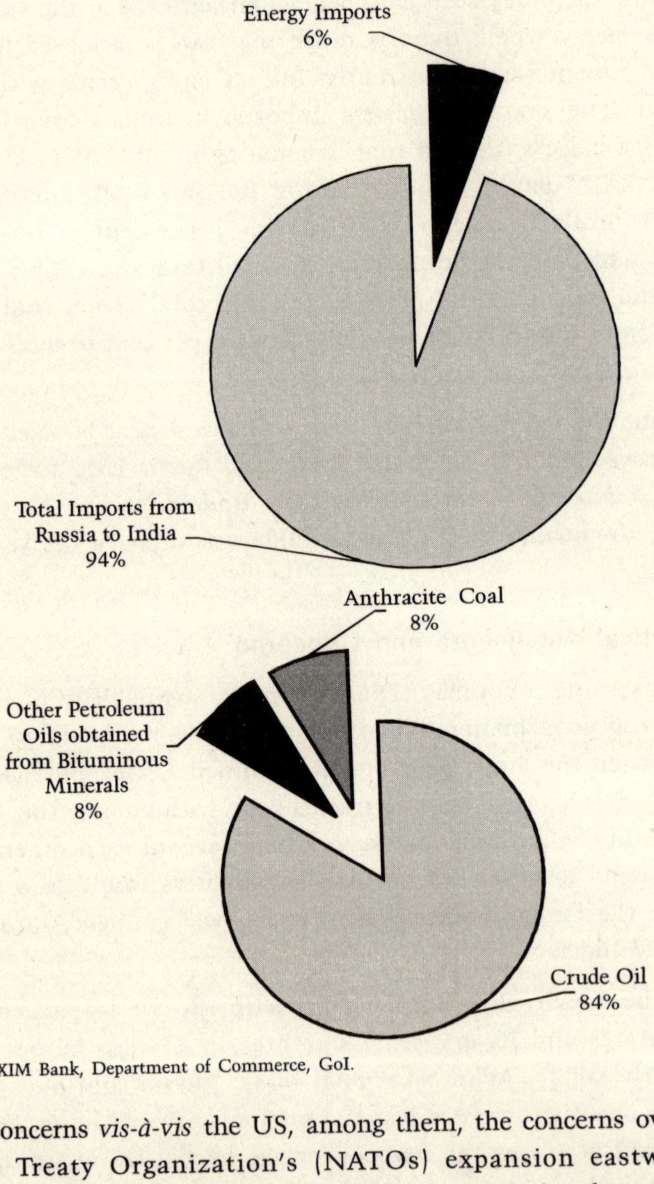

Source: EXIM Bank, Department of Commerce, GoI.

myriad concerns *vis-à-vis* the US, among them, the concerns over North Atlantic Treaty Organization's (NATOs) expansion eastwards (to Ukraine and Georgia), talks by the US to extend the theatre missile defence (TMD) to the Czech Republic and Poland, and also US backing for the Baku-Tbilisi-Ceyhan (BTC) pipeline that seeks to circumvent Russia in order to give access to Western Europe and the US to Caspian oil. As India tries to work out possibilities to gain access to oil reserves in the Caspian region and Central Asia, the dynamics between Eastern Europe, the Caspian countries, Russia and the US will need to be kept in mind. India's dire energy needs imply that India will need to continue exercising a pragmatic foreign policy that is capable of balancing competing interests and compulsions. That is, the good relations between the US and India must continue to be treated at par with relations with Russia.

India's energy linkages with Russia as well as the Central Asian Republics (CARs) would be to a great extent, influenced by Russia and India's relations with China as well as the CARs. China has often been perceived as India's chief competitor in the context of access to energy. This is magnified by the fact, that India is not as far ahead of the 'game' as China is, particularly in garnering access to 'new' energy rich countries in Central Asia. Also, given its proximity to Russia, China is at a distinct advantage at deepening its energy imports from Russia, as compared to India. Given the fact, that India is far removed from access to these energy-rich regions, it needs to look at collaborative mechanisms that afford win-win outcomes rather than competitive out-bidding and undercutting. To this end, India's observer status at the Shanghai Cooperation Organisation (SCO), which represents most of the CARs (excluding Turkmenistan), Russia as well as China, is a positive development. Joint energy projects in the oil and gas sector, as well as exploration of new hydrocarbon reserves is already a key priority area of the SCO.[2] India must continue to engage with the SCO and support joint projects in which it could also have a stake with the other countries. Another key multilateral organisation that can be seen as providing an impetus to India's energy linkages with Russia as well as China, is the China-India-Russia Strategic Triangle. Although the organisation is motivated by more esoteric pronouncements on important global issues such as Kosovo, Iran, Afghanistan and terrorism, on several occasions in the past the three countries have suggested energy as an area for greater cooperation.

Therefore, while there are clearly challenges at the geopolitical level, there are also key levers that India and Russia can use to ensure engagement at the broader geopolitical level, as well as in the context of energy.

Secure Routes

The availability of affordable energy means little if there is no accessibility or if the cost of access is prohibitive. When it comes to Russia, the biggest obstacle to enhancing the energy dimension of the partnership is precisely this—the absence of viable routes for the supply of energy. The present route, that India uses to trade with Russia is long and circuitous. It is for this reason that Russia will not, despite best intentions, emerge as a big energy partner for India unless and until some alternative mechanisms and routes are identified or worked out on the ground.

From St. Petersburg to the nearest port on India's west coast (Cochin), it takes about 22 days and 9 hours to cover a distance of 7,516 nautical miles. This route must pass through the Gulf of Aden, the Suez, through the Mediterranean, and the North Sea, the Baltic Sea and through the Gulf of Finland and into St. Petersburg. However, the Gulf of Aden and the coast off Somalia have become increasingly notorious for pirate attacks. The hijacking of the Sirius Star late in 2008, demonstrates that secure routes free of piracy are equally important for the energy security of any country. The Sirius Star was said to have been carrying US$ 110 million of crude oil bound for America, owned by Saudi Aramco.

The second route that India can examine to source energy from Russia, if and when East Siberia's oil and gas comes online, is the shipping route from Vladivostok to India's east coast (Chennai). This route is far shorter—about 4,569 nautical miles and a transit time of 13 days and 14 hours. However, this route must pass through the Malacca Straits—a chokepoint which is also pirate-infested. At its narrowest, the Strait is merely 1.7 miles, thereby making passing tankers a ready target for thefts and hijackings, particularly because these tankers are slow-moving and difficult to manoeuvre. Vessels carrying LNG are even more difficult to steer, given the inflammable nature of the cargo. Over

200 ships pass the Malacca Straits everyday. About half of the world's oil and two-thirds of the world's LNG passes through the Malacca Straits. Not only piracy, but terrorist outfits and rebel insurgent groups operating in the region make the Straits a particularly insecure and risky sea lane of communication (SLOC) for energy imports.

There are two alternative arrangements that offer a way out for India to access Russian energy. However, these suggestions are neither new nor easy to work out. One of these alternatives is the International North-South Transport Corridor (INSTC). The INSTC is a multi-modal transportation agreement that was established on 12 September 2000 in St. Petersburg, by Iran, Russia and India for the purpose of promoting transportation cooperation. The corridor stretches from ports in India across the Arabian Sea to the southern Iranian port of Bandar Abbas, where goods then transit Iran and the Caspian Sea to ports in Russia's sector of the Caspian. From there, the route stretches along the Volga River via Moscow to northern Europe. When, and if, the corridor becomes a reality, it could slash costs and shipment times considerably. At present, it costs US$ 3,500 to ship goods to India.

Another alternative method that could be attempted is to enter into swap arrangements. This has already been suggested several times in the past, but has eluded agreement between the concerned countries. For example, a deal to swap natural gas with Japan has been on the table. According to this arrangement, Japan's imports from West Asia could be swapped by supplies of gas from India's stakes in Sakhalin-I. However, these talks have fallen through in the past, primarily due to Japan's perceptions of Russia as an unreliable energy partner. Japan was unhappy about the way Japanese companies had to let go of their stake in Sakhalin-II under pressure from the Russian government. Had the deal come through, it would have substantially cut the transportation costs and the landed price of gas to both India and Japan.

Risk Ratings

The security of energy supplies is as important for a country as is access and availability of energy. In order to ensure the security of supplies, countries need to assess the relative stability and risks involved in sourcing energy supplies from a particular energy-rich country. Russia's position as a secure energy supplier, therefore, depends on an assessment of relative risks and the stability of the country. However, an assessment of the risks (arising from domestic sources of instability as well as the degree of openness of the Russian economy) needs to be arrived at independently—from an Indian standpoint and not through Western eyes.

In terms of political risk ratings, Russia is ranked as relatively risky by Western risk rating agencies, particularly on the basis of parameters such as government stability, law and order situation and ethnic tensions. However, Russia does not have unlimited capacity to convert its energy muscle into real political influence. There are differing agendas within the country. Furthermore, Russia is not as much of a monolith as it is touted to be in the Western media. These are some of the caveats that India must heed when assessing Russia.

In terms of the economic risks involved, in the World Bank's 'Doing Business' rankings such as ease of doing business, trading across borders, enforcing contracts and so on, Russia scores a low in the first two, but fairs better in terms of starting a business and enforcing contracts. However, risk taking is perhaps a subjective factor for companies and countries. Irrespective of these ratings and rankings, it is the experience that comes from being engaged, that is, at the end of the day capable of overriding concerns arising from domestic sources of instability and risk. Risk-averseness is relative to the relative demand and rise in import dependency. Thus, as parameters to gauge whether Russia is a favourable energy partner for India or not, risk ratings would and should play a relatively minor role as compared to other parameters analysed.

The Prognosis

An expansion of energy linkages between Russia and India have to be seen as part of the broader trade and political relations between the two. In order to build stable and enduring energy relations, a consistent effort needs to be made in building mutually beneficial stakes and networks, particularly in the trade and investment sector. Given the fact that the energy calculus has made international alignments more nebulous, India will need to continue working towards building energy partnerships with countries that might not be on a sound wicket with each other.

Furthermore, India will need to work out a balance between its energy needs and compulsions with larger geopolitical concerns and power configurations at the regional/international level. To achieve this, regional frameworks and dialogues need to be in place in order to engineer a collaborative approach to energy security and the access to energy-rich regions or countries. It is clear that distance and the absence of cost-effective transportation routes are the biggest obstacles that India faces in expanding its energy linkages with Russia. Therefore, swap arrangements and joint energy projects offer a distinct advantage to India; for which collaboration and regional dialogues are of tremendous use. In the end, what need to be kept in mind is that Russia will never be India's main energy partner and nor will India be a key destination for Russian energy. However, as India grows, import dependencies rise and a greater cost to carbon is attached, access to any amount of energy (oil, natural gas, uranium and even coal) will go a longer way in alleviating the energy crunch that India will feel in the future. Therefore, Russia is a definite choice and a favourable one at that for India to focus its energies on. However, there is a dire need to put other important levers in place which could help enhance India's energy linkages with Russia. Both countries need to focus on developing these levers in the coming years such as secure route options, swap arrangements and greater trade and bilateral linkages.

End Notes

1. OECD, NEA & IAEA (2007). "The reasonably assured resources plus inferred resources, to US$ 130/kg U", January 1, *Uranium 2007: Resources, Production and Demand* ("Red Book"), Available at: *http://www.world-nuclear.org/info/inf75.html*
2. Russia mooted the idea of the "SCO Energy Club" in 2007, although the other members have been slow in committing to this.

References

Energy Information Analysis (2008). "Russia", available at: *www.eia.doe.gov/cabs/russia.html* - 20k, Accessed on 23 February 2009.

Legvold, Robert (2008). "Russia's strategic vision and the role of energy", *NBR Analysis* 19(2): 9-22.

Planning Commission (2006). *Integrated Energy Policy*. Report of the Expert Committee. Available at: *http://planningcommission.nic.in/reports/genrep/rep_intengy.pdf*, Accessed on 5 March 2009.

Reuters (2007a). "Russia coal exports to start falling", 6 June, Available at: *http://uk.reuters.com/article/electionsNews/idUKL0638050320070608*, Accessed on 22 February 2009.

———. (2007b). "Russia exporters eye India as new steam coal market", 11 September, Available at: *http://in.reuters.com/article/businessNews/idINIndia-29459820070911*, Accessed on 22 February 2009.

RusEnergy (2005). "Oil refining needs sizeable investments", 25 March, Available at: *http://rusenergy.blogspot.com/2005/03/oil-refining-needs-sizeable.html*, Accessed on 24 February 2009.

Sasi, Anil (2008). "India hopes to leverage edge in reactors, thorium technology", *The Hindu Business Line*, 7 September, Available at: *http://www.blonnet.com/2008/09/07/stories/2008090751300300.htm*, Accessed on 22 February 2009.

Sinha, Amitabh (2009). "India signs uranium contract with Russia", *The Indian Express*, 11 February, Available at: *http://www.expressindia.com/latest-news/India-to-sign-uranium-purchase-contract-with-Russia/422044/*, Accessed on 22 February 2009.

TERI (2006). *National Energy Map for India. Technology Vision 2030*. Office of the Principal Adviser, Government of India.

The Economist (2008). "Russia economy: Closer to OPEC", *The Economist*, 3 November.

5 India-Russia Civil Nuclear Cooperation

G. Balachandran

India had recognised the useful role of nuclear science in the economic development of a nation as early as 1948 thanks to the vision of scientists like Dr. Homi Bhabha and statesmen like Pandit Jawaharlal Nehru. In fact as early as 1944, Dr. Bhabha had written a letter to Sir Dorabji Tata Trust proposing the foundation of an institute devoted to fundamental research observing that "when nuclear energy has been successfully applied for power production, in say a couple of decades from now, India will not have to look abroad for its experts but will find them ready at home." It was not surprising, therefore, with the full support of the then Prime Minister Nehru, nuclear science was given a prominent place in Indian science and technology future. An Atomic Energy Committee (AEC) was set up at the end of 1945, even before India attained Independence and the first Atomic Energy Bill was passed as early as April 1948 and the first Atomic Energy Commission was constituted in August 1948. Thereafter in quick succession in 1950, the Indian Rare Earths Limited (IRE), owned by the Government of India was set up for recovering minerals, processing of rare earths compounds and thorium-uranium concentrates. A separate Department of Atomic Energy was created in 1954.

While developing indigenous scientific and technological capabilities, India was not unmindful of building relationships with other nations in the field of nuclear science. Asia's first research reactor, Apsara, reached criticality in August 1956. It was built with the assistance of the United Kingdom Atomic Energy Authority (UKAEA). A second 40 MWt research reactor, CIRUS, built with Canadian assistance reached criticality in July 1960.

During this period India had entered into nuclear cooperation agreements, both for research and development efforts and supply of materials with a number of countries. Some of the earliest research and development cooperation agreements were signed with Hungary in August 1961 and USSR in October 1961 and many more since then.

In respect of nuclear cooperation on material transfers, the first agreement was with the US in March 1956 for transfer of heavy water for CIRUS, with the India-Canada agreement for the CIRUS project being concluded in April 1956. Thereafter, India entered into an agreement with USA in August 1963 for the supply and construction of a nuclear power plant—the two units of 220 MWe each at Tarapur, followed by a similar agreement with Canada in December 1963 for the supply of two pressurised heavy water reactors (PHWRs) at Rajasthan Atomic Power Station (RAPS), each with a capacity of 220 MWe.

However, subsequent to the first Indian nuclear test in 1974, nuclear cooperation between India and US, and India and Canada came to an end. For the running of the two nuclear power reactors, India entered into a series of nuclear cooperation agreements with other nations—with the then USSR in September 1976 for the supply of heavy water for RAPS; with France in November 1982 for the supply of enriched uranium fuel for Tarapur followed by subsequent fuel supply agreements for Tarapur with China and Russia. India and Russia also entered into an agreement in 1988 for the supply of two light water reactors, of 1000 MWe capacity each, to be commissioned at Koodankulam in South India.

However, with the tightening of the Supply Guidelines by the Nuclear Suppliers Group (NSG) in April 1993, India's civil nuclear cooperation with other nations and in particular with NSG member countries came to an end.

It was only after the India-US nuclear cooperation agreement of July 2005 that negotiations began on the relaxation of NSG guidelines, specifically with respect to the requirement of full scope safeguards for international civil nuclear cooperation between India and the NSG members. The NSG finally amended their guidelines to allow for nuclear commerce with India on September 6, 2008.

India-Russia Civil Nuclear Cooperation

India/USSR and India-Russia civil nuclear cooperation, while longstanding, has not been without its ups and downs. As mentioned earlier, the first nuclear scientific and technical cooperation agreement was signed in 1961. Much later, in 1976, the first nuclear supply agreement was signed for the supply of heavy water for the two PHWRs in Rajasthan built with Canadian assistance.

India had needed assistance for the running of both the two US supplied Tarapur Atomic Power Station (TAPS) reactors and the two Canadian supplied Rajasthan Atomic Power Plant (RAPP) reactors—the former for the supply of enriched uranium fuel for its operations and a one-time supply of heavy water for the latter. At that time, in line with the international nuclear commerce conventions, India had entered into safeguards agreements with the International Atomic Energy Agency (IAEA) in respect of both TAPS and RAPP.

When India entered into fresh supply agreements with substitute suppliers in lieu of US and Canada, it had to enter into fresh safeguards agreements for these supplies.

While the new safeguards agreement, as a result of the supply of enriched uranium fuel for TAPS did not impose any additional conditionalities on India, the safeguards agreement as a result of a one-time supply of heavy water by the then USSR, imposed far stricter conditions on India than was in the original RAPP safeguards agreement concluded at the time of the Canadian agreement.

None of the conditions of safeguards in the original TAPS safeguards agreement were modified except to include France as the fuel supplier. However, the modified RAPP safeguards agreements, as a result of the supply of heavy water by USSR, substantially altered the terms of the original RAPP safeguards agreement. In particular, it subjected RAPP to perpetual safeguards even though RAPP ceased to have any USSR supplied heavy water for its operations. The perpetuity and pursuit clauses of the safeguards were made applicable even after RAPP ceased to require any imported heavy water or fuel for its operations. On the other hand, in case of TAPS, it effectively ceases to be under safeguards if it operates on indigenous fuel.

In effect, the nuclear transfer practice of USSR was far stricter than that of either the US or Canada. In fact, this aspect of the USSR/Russia practice of being stricter than NSG members continued well into the 1990s.

Thus, for example, while the NSG amended their supply guidelines to require fullscope safeguards from the recipient countries only in April 1993, Russia by a Presidential Edict (Presidential Edict 312) made fullscope safeguards as a precondition for nuclear suppliers as early as March 1992. Then again while the 1993 NSG amendment to its guidelines allowed for transfers in exceptional cases when deemed essential for the safe operation of existing safeguarded facilities, Russia amended its domestic laws (Presidential Edict 312 of 1992) to include such transfers only in 2000.

India-Russia Nuclear Cooperation: Post-Yeltsin Era

However, it must be admitted that while the USSR/Russia nuclear supply rules and regulations were stricter than the NSG norms—which had been specifically targeted against India—from 2000 onwards the Russian attitude towards civil nuclear cooperation with India changed in a dramatic fashion. The 2000 amendment to Russian laws was in specific response to the Indian request for fuel for TAPS operations. Russia faced intense hostility from other NSG members as a result of its supply of fuel for TAPS under the safety exemption clause, when the other NSG members had refused such fuel supply. Russia stood steadfast and went ahead with the fuel supply. Thereafter, in the subsequent year, Russia proposed that NSG create a new type of membership in the group-associate membership, and suggested India as a candidate. However, the Russian proposal did not find favour with the other NSG members and the idea was dropped.

Although the original Koodankulum agreement was signed in 1988, actual contracts for the reactors were finalised much later in early 1990s after the amendment to NSG guidelines. Russia also went ahead with the 1998 agreement for the two reactors at Koodankulam even though it came under some criticism from other NSG members for allegedly breaching the NSG guidelines. Russia, however, stood its ground and justified the supply as predating the NSG amendment.

In addition, although NSG guidelines do not make any reference to nuclear transfers in respect of naval vessels, Russia agreed to lease India a nuclear submarine, first time that such a transfer had been made to a non-nuclear weapon state.

Further, post the July 2005 India-US joint statement of nuclear cooperation, Russia agreed to a fresh supply of fuel for TAPS even before the NSG amended its guidelines, once again under the safety exemption clause.

The Future of India-Russia Civil Nuclear Cooperation

The future of India-Russia civil nuclear cooperation depends much on the manner in which both conduct their bilateral and multilateral diplomacy in the coming years.

On the positive side, post-1998 Indian nuclear tests Russia while being critical of the tests, did not suspend the ongoing Koodankulum contract or suspend fuel supplies. Also, while the India-Russia nuclear cooperation agreement has not been made public, it is understood—subject to correction—that the agreement allows India to reprocess the spent fuel from Russian reactors, as probably also the spent fuel from the use of Russian fuel at TAPS. It is further understood that the agreement does not include any requirement for suspension of nuclear supplies except in case of violation of IAEA safeguards by India. Further, subsequent to the 2008 NSG amendment to its guidelines for nuclear transfer, India and Russia have entered into an agreement for additional supply of reactors at Koodankulum. These are positive signs for a healthy relationship between the two countries in the sphere of nuclear energy.

The Presidential Edict 312 of 1992 and its 2000 amendment had not removed the requirement of fullscope safeguards from Russian laws. This was done only in February 2009, much after the NSG amendment. However, the February 16, 2002 amendment has relaxed the conditions for India-Russia nuclear cooperation far more than the NSG amendment. While the NSG amendment is only in respect of supplies of reactors and fuel, the Russian amendment goes much further by allowing "The export from the Russian Federation to India of nuclear materials, as well as technology, equipment and special non-nuclear materials related to their processing, use and their production, can be conducted only if these materials are used in nuclear installations, under the IAEA monitoring."

This is in sharp contrast to the recommendation, contentious and yet to be ratified, recommendation made by the NSG Consultative Committee (CG) in November 2007 that Enrichment and Reprocessing (ENR) technologies should be supplied only to those countries that have signed the NPT and have fullscope safeguards on all their nuclear activities—a condition that would automatically disqualify India. Indeed, it is apparent that this amendment to NSG guidelines was dictated solely to act against India. While this amendment to NSG guidelines was proposed in November 2008, the much relaxed laws in respect to India enacted by Russia was made in February 2009.

While this would indicate a positive approach from Russia towards civil nuclear commerce with India, the recent G8 declaration, to which Russia was also a party, stated "To reduce the proliferation risks associated with the spread of enrichment and reprocessing facilities, equipment and technology, we welcome the progress that continues to be made by the Nuclear Suppliers Group (NSG) on mechanisms to strengthen controls on transfers of such enrichment and reprocessing items and technology. While noting that the NSG has not yet reached consensus on this issue, we agree that the NSG discussions have yielded useful and constructive proposals contained in the NSG's 'clean text' developed at the 20 November 2008 Consultative Group meeting. Pending completion of work in the NSG, we agree to implement this text on a national basis in the next year."

It is not clear how Russia will reconcile its G8 position with its current laws. If it amends its domestic laws once again to conform to its G8 position, then there can be no technology commerce between India and Russia on ENR technologies. If it does not want to discriminate against India on NPT status basis, then it will have to disagree to a consensus decision at NSG on the ENR technology transfer item.

It would, of course, help matters immensely if India and Russia were to conclude an umbrella agreement on ENR technology transfer now itself, leaving the details to be worked out later. In that case, even if NSG were to amend the guidelines to prohibit ENR technology transfers to non-NPT countries, Russia can claim the grandfather clause exemption, usually available to NSG members when amendments are made to NSG guidelines, and still maintain its good relations with India. It is, of course, too early to speculate how this issue will progress in the coming months. If this matter i.e., ENR technology transfer is settled in a bilaterally positive manner, there is vast scope for India-Russia cooperation in civil nuclear activities. These include:

1) India-Russia nuclear cooperation agreement including:
   a. Transfer of nuclear power reactors including the technology of such reactors.
   b. Fuel supply agreement for both supplied reactors and other reactors operating in India, including both natural uranium and enriched uranium.
   c. Right to reprocess spent fuel.
   d. Fuel supply assurance under all circumstances.
   e. In principle agreement to transfer reprocessing technology and enrichment technology.
2) Operationalisation of 1961 nuclear cooperation agreement involving research connected with the development of atomic power reactors using natural uranium, breeder reactors using plutonium as well as research on the thorium-uranium-233 cycle.
3) Involving India as part of RTF (Radkowsky Thorium Fuel) cycle project—a cooperative research project currently involving Russia, US and Israel.
4) Involving India as a partner in the International Uranium Enrichment Center (IUEC) at Angarsk without requiring India to forgo development of weapon-related sensitive nuclear technologies.

Section II
India-Russian Economic Cooperation

6 Economic Subsystem of Russia-India Relations

Lounev Sergey Ivanovich

Russia and India are natural and objective friends.[1] The logic of geopolitics dictates that the two nations would strengthen their relationship further. India can be a reliable partner in the case of actualisation of the threat to Russian security from the South. If, for instance, we take the southern boundaries of Russia, India is already playing a very positive role as her opposition to Pakistan limits the activity of the latter in the zone. India is a good partner for Russia in the military field. The development of military-political subsystem of bilateral relations is important for India as well.

There are practically no differences between the two countries on the vast majority of world problems. What is especially important is that the possibility of establishing a unipolar world is unacceptable to both countries. Further, broadening of the use of violence, a policy of the North, will inevitably lead to the strengthening of relations between Russia and India. They oppose the monopolistic position of the North and its present policy. But, no one wants to challenge the North to an open fight. Moreover, the overall strengthening of the economic links with the North has become one of the major features of India and Russia from the beginning of the nineties. Both countries understand the necessity to at least maintain normal relations with the West. The reduction of tension between the North and the South is profitable to Russia and India. The role of a mediator, and bridge, between the developed and developing countries would be favourable for them. They have the same goals in respect to the Islamic world as well. It is vital to: a) normalise relations with the region; b) oppose the attempts of certain Western forces to impose on the countries, the role of the vanguard in the struggle against the Muslim world; and c) to fight decisively against Islamic extremists.

The existence of ethnic and religious separatists causes Russia and India to adopt a similar approach to the problem of so-called self-determination, terrorism and separatism. It is necessary to point out the relative closeness of the two countries in the sphere of cultural life: spiritualism, this immanent element of their civilisations, opposes the materialism and consumerism of the developed countries.

One cannot help stressing the unanimity of the complexity of tasks facing Russia and India in the sphere of foreign economy. Both the countries have to aim at integrating into the world economy, as in increasing their competitiveness, even while maintaining a degree of protectionism. The joint goals of Russia and India result not only from their analogous place in the world economy, but from the vastness of their territory and population as well. It is not a coincidence that in November 2008 in Rio de Janeiro, the Russian President, Dmitry Medvedev, identified India as well as China among Moscow's key partners in the creation of a new multilateral global financial order and security architecture.[2]

There are good relations between Russia and India at the grassroot level. The public opinion surveys show that Russia is still among the most popular countries in India and vice versa. In the beginning of 2009, 39 per cent Indians expressed a positive view of Russian influence in the world (though 74 per cent Chinese occupied this position); the Russian attitude towards India is positive (48 per cent). The number of Russians that had a negative view of India was small, while it was significant against Europe (54 per cent against Germans, 50 per cent against Frenchmen and 47 per cent against Spaniards).[3]

But there are some obstacles facing the development of bilateral links between the two countries. There is a need to mention, for example, the problem of both the countries' elites. The pro-Western (and specifically, pro-American) forces are becoming increasingly influential in India. There is not a member of the Indian elite who does not have relatives or close friends in the United States (US). Certain political leaders are obsessed with the might of US and appeals for orientation exclusively towards the US. This unhindered spread of Western ideas may lead to the crash of Indian traditional consensus on foreign policy that lays utmost stress on pursuing an independent political course.

But the Russian elite is also on the whole still pro-Western. This is evident from the growth of anti-Americanism, but not of anti-Europeanism. Hence, the idea has been propagated (rather naïve) about the possible split between the USA (United States of America) and Europe, and about Russia being the partner of Europe.[4] One can only hope that the recent reaction of Europe to the events in Georgia will sober the Russian elite. The current Russian foreign policy emphasises on the uniqueness of Russian geopolitical, historic and cultural position as a "bridge" between Europe and Asia. The idea is to take advantage of these special features and enrich Russia by establishing ties both with the North and the South.

The economic subsystem of the bilateral relations is the weakest. The overall strengthening of economic links with the North has become one of the main directions of both countries since the beginning of the 1990s. It is clear that economic cooperation is the best way to achieve trust between the two countries. Moreover, comprehensive development of economic ties may even overweigh political, military and cultural differences and could help to build some kind of confidence. Take, for example, the relations between China and Japan, China and the USA.

It is clear that if Russia-India economic subsystem is not strengthened then the whole complex of our mutually beneficial ties in the other spheres will be severely weakened. May be not in the near future, but in some 15 years they may unfortunately happen. That is why, it is necessary to find some ways to develop Russian-Indian economic ties.

The influential Indian business community has made no secret of its antagonism towards socialism. It was the only segment of Indian society that was satisfied with the break-up of the USSR. Now Indian business on the whole is not particularly interested in the rapprochement with Russia. The same can be said of Russian business. In such conditions, it is necessary to restore some form of state economic ties, on the one hand, and to stimulate business to develop bilateral ties, on the other. For example, it is possible to give some state guarantees to Indian businessmen in Russia, and similar guarantees to Russian businessmen in India. It is necessary that the state lobby the interests of private business in the partner-country on a reciprocal basis.

There are no great prospects for promoting trade relations for the time being. In the 1990s, the volume of trade between Russia and India ($1.2-1.8 billion) dropped by several times compared to the 1980s. The volume amounted to $1.3 billion in 2002/03, $1.67 billion 2003/04, $1.95 billion in 2004/05, $2.76 billion in 2005/06, $3.41 billion 2006/07 and $3.51 billion 2007/08.[5] The Foreign Ministry of Russia gave the figure of $7 billion for 2008.[6] But evidently the figures of military sales were included. It will be very difficult to realise the aim of increasing the volume of trade to $10 billion by 2010.

Unfortunately, the level of our mutual trade is objectively limited. Geographical factors play a negative role: very long sea route considerably raise the price of transportation. The only way out is to develop the "North–South" (Russia–Iran–India) transport corridor. According to estimates, we may save up to 20 per cent in transportation cost with the use of this route. It may be of special importance for Russia and India for transportation of goods from South-East Asia to Europe. But the project is being implemented extremely slowly.

But there are other economic spheres that have a huge development potential. The sphere of energy is the most important. The prospect of a strategic and inexpensive energy supply from Russia to India (China and Japan as well) provides a major opportunity for increased regional integration involving energy companies, investors and governments. It is a key part of the vision for a more integrated Asia.

Analysts predict that for the next 25 years, the per capita GDP of India will increase by 5 per cent per annum. Many researchers think that in 10 years, India's GDP, calculated on purchasing power capacity, will practically equal that of Japan. This means that energy consumption in India will increase year by year. According to the Paris-based International Energy Association, the total energy consumption in

India is projected to increase by 2.6 per cent per annum, from 13 quadrillion Bthu in 2003 to 23.5 quadrillion Bthu in 2025.[7]

Oil and gas are the world's foremost source of primary energy consumption, and Russia may play a very important role in supplying India and other Asian giants with hydrocarbons. India accounted for 12.5 per cent of total primary energy consumption in the Asia Pacific region. Oil and gas currently meet about 42 per cent of energy consumption of the country. It is estimated that they will account for half the energy consumption by the end of the first quarter of the 21st century. In 2007, the level of domestic production of crude oil in India amounted to 880,500 bbl per day and oil consumption amounted to 2.722 million bbl per day. In that year, natural gas production was equal to 31.7 billion standard cubic metres, and its consumption amounted to 41.7 billion standard cubic metres.[8] According to the calculations of the International Energy Association, India's oil consumption is projected to increase in the first quarter of the century by 4 per cent per annum and gas consumption by 6 per cent.[9]

It is evident from the figures that India will have to diversify its sources of oil and gas import, because energy import implies vulnerability to external prices' shocks and supply fluctuations, which threaten the country's energy security. India's primary energy consumption is dominated by coal. But the growth of coal production has its limits. Moreover, adverse environmental impact of coal is a major issue. Another is the dependence of India on one major source of supply, the Middle East, a turbulent zone with ceaseless internal and external conflicts.

As for alternative sources of energy, there are three situational scenarios in this region. First, the United States will wholly check the activities of the radicals in the Middle East. In that case, the energy security of India, and of Asia as a whole, will be dominated by the USA.

Second, the growth of terrorist activities in the region will endanger the supply of energy from this region.

Third, the status quo may exist for a short period of time with fluctuations from the second to the third scenario, as noted above.

Hence, it is necessary for India to search for alternative sources of energy supply. Many experts are pointing out to Central Asia as a supplier of oil and gas. But the volume of such reserves in this region is exaggerated. For example, proven reserves of oil and gas in the Caspian Basin (including Russian and Iranian sectors) approximately comprise 3 per cent of the world reserves. For comparison, one may note that reserves of the Persian Gulf in oil are 18 times bigger, and in gas 6 times bigger. So, even in the long run, the Caspian Sea will not be transformed into the Persian Gulf.

There are huge problems in the transportation of oil and gas from Central Asia. As an example: Turkmenistan had four projects to construct gas pipelines; all four projects were not realised, and in 2003 Turkmenistan signed a contract concerning the largest part of gas exports with Russia.

That does not mean that Central Asia as provider of the major portion of its gas to Russia should be ignored as a energy supplier. But it is evident that investments in oil and gas production are at the moment the only economically viable proposition in the area. There are, of course some variations, like joint ventures with Russia for oil and gas production in the region.

By the end of 2006, the first tanker brought to India 90 thousand tonnes of Sakhalin oil; 20 more tankers came in 2007 that raised the volume of trade. Some experts consider that it is possible for India to receive 50 million tonnes of Russian oil annually. Russian, Indian and Chinese experts have begun to promote the project which involves the construction of an oil pipeline from Russia to India via China (though Russian specialists are cautious about the possibility of the project being realised).

In November 2008, the Petroleum and Natural Gas Minister, Murli Deora, made a very successful visit to Moscow. Russia has agreed, in principle, to India making investments in Russian oil and gas sectors (formation of joint venture between ONGC Videsh Limited (OVL) and Rosneft or Gazprom for taking up exploration and development projects in east Siberia; participation in Sakhalin-III and IV projects).[10] India has expressed an interest in the purchase of LNG. Japan already imports gas in liquefied form. Russia can guarantee the supply of liquefied gas for a very long time, which is an important factor in energy security.

By collaborating with Russia, India will benefit as follows:

1) Diversification of the import of gas and oil that will strengthen energy security;
2) Become more independent world leader;
3) Secure a long-term reliable defence supplier;
4) Strengthen bilateral relations;
5) Improvement of the ecological situation;
6) Intensification of regional integration.

The cooperation in the atomic energy sector is also important. From 2002, Russia began the construction of two reactors for the atomic power station at Koodankulam and promised to provide fuel to these reactors for life. During the last visit of Manmohan Singh to Moscow, both sides agreed that Russia would construct four more reactors at Koodankulam. During the visit of President Medvedev to India in December 2008, the official agreement was signed.

India is going to spend $100 billion for the construction of atomic power stations and Russia is to play a major part in this project. The Indo-American agreement signed in 2006 has created negative reactions in Russia. On the one hand, USA and France have become serious competitors in Indian market. On the other hand, the rigid stand of Washington prevented Russian-Indian ties in this sphere from developing. For example, the agreement on Koodankulam was ready by 1994, but was signed only by the end of 2001.

There are also good prospects for mutual cooperation in such fields as heat and power engineering and hydropower engineering, the construction of highways and underground railways in India, modernisation of the metallurgical works, coal mining and engineering industry. There are big plans in India for the construction and reconstruction of enterprises in thermal and hydropower production, civil use of nuclear energy, aviation, desalination of water etc. This sphere of cooperation could be a mutually beneficial one. But it is necessary to point out that Russia loses many contracts in India to Western companies. To a certain extent, it is the result of negative information about Russia that appears in Indian media from Western sources.

The scientific-industrial sphere is extremely important. Now there are more than 300 joint projects of applied and fundamental nature (mathematics, mechanics, chemistry, physics, science of materials, electronics, oceanography, seismology, information technology, bioengineering, space, pharmaceutics, etc.) under implementation in the framework of long-term programme for scientific cooperation. But it is not enough.

India and Russia are super large countries in terms of quantitative indicators. From the point of view of qualitative characteristics, the countries are in different categories. India can hardly transit to the post-industrial stage of development. The huge number of poor makes no sense of effective models for developed countries. For instance, there is not much sense in applying new resource preserving technologies, while it is not obvious where the released working force should go; thus, it is not a mere coincidence, that the majority of technological achievements of India are export-oriented. The vivid example is India's software production. Achievements are great, but we should take into consideration that practically 90 per cent of India's software is exported. Its consumption in India is very limited. But India is developing effectively on the industrial path of development.

Russia has certain opportunities to develop a "knowledge economy" (high technology and science related production) and choose the post-industrial way of development.

There are three theoretical models of development: post-industrial country, industrial country and resource country.

Development as a resource country (in other words as a village of the world) may be profitable one for some time. But the end will be tragic. It will be the end of the country because according to estimates, it is necessary to restrict the population in Russia to 12-13 million so that it can function as a resource base for the world economy. If Russia chooses this way, it will lead to degradation of the country.

The path of industrial development is also closed to Russia because in a modern globalised world Russia may not be able to face competition mainly due to the objective reasons: vast territory, lack of infrastructure and severe climate. As a consequence, Russian products will be at least 10-15 per cent more expensive than those of other countries.

Hence, there is only one way for Russia: post-industrial way of development. It means development of high technology, the composition of science and production and other such developments. Russia still has good potential to move in this direction because of its solid foundations in science, and fundamental science in particular.

The diversity of the situation in Russia and India can produce wonderful results. The combination of Russian potential in high technology and availability of 30 per cent of the world resources, with India's standing in the fields of industry and engineering, could result in major achievements. For example in the sphere of software. Analysis shows that India is advanced in certain segments of software. In the case of Russia, its achievements belong to the higher segment of software-related technologies. Some people speak about competition between Russia and India in this sphere, but I see no competition. Actually it is necessary to combine efforts because the niches are different. The best results could be achieved if we combine Russian fundamental sciences related to software and India's achievements in engineering. Moreover, it would be great to include the third factor, the qualitative and inexpensive Chinese workforce. If this is realised, both India and Russia might confront a paradoxical situation. The Russian economic standards will move closer to the North as a result of its development of political and economic connections with the South.

Joint investments deserve priority. Today, Russian investments in the Indian economy are rather modest. But Russian companies show keen interest in different spheres, especially in telecommunications, information technologies, aluminium industry, and the energy sector. For example, Russia had invested $250 million in a titanium project in Orissa and would extend $200 million to build the capacity in a heavy-duty bearing plant in Hyderabad. Investment conglomerate Systema, having acquired a stake in Shyam Telecom in 2007, is ready to invest up to $7 billion in the next two years for modernisation of mobile services.[11] Gazprom's subsidiary, Transgas invested in 26 blocks of the strategic gas pipeline between Vijayawada and Ahmedabad.[12] Rosneft is ready to invest in ONGC project in Mangalore. Indian investments are bigger, about $2 billion, but again we speak about only two projects: Sakhalin-1 oil project (OVL has 20 per cent stake in Sakhalin-I fields fetching the nation 2.4 million tonnes of crude annually) and the Sun group brewery project. But the latest negotiations of Mr. Murli Deora will raise this sum considerably.

There are good prospects for the creation of Indo-Russian joint ventures in the third countries (Central Asia, foremost) with regard to agricultural sphere, joint development of mineral, energy and timber resources of Siberia and Russia. The Far East can also become an important arena of Indo-Russian cooperation.

If nothing is done in the sphere of Russian-Indian economic subsystem, the complex of mutual ties will become weak (may be not in the near future but in 10-15 years). But the economic subsystem of the bilateral relations can develop positively if both governments show political will.

End Notes

1. For more details see Gleriy, Shirokov and Lounev Sergey (1998). *Russia, China and India in the Modern Global Processes*. Moscow: Moscow Public Science Foundation; Sergey, Lounev (1999). *The Challenges to the Security of the Southern Boundaries of Russia*. Moscow: Moscow Public Science Foundation; Sergey, Lounev and Shirokov Gleriy (2001). *Transformation of the World System: The Role of Largest States of Eurasia*. Moscow: Academia; Sergey, Lounev and Khoros Vladimir (2005). *Indian Civilization in the Globalizing World*. Moscow: Institute of World Economy and International Relations; Sergey, Lounev (2006). *India: Foreign Policy and Economy*. Moscow State Institute (University) of International Relations.
2. Statements for the Press after Russian-Brazilian Talks, *http://www.kremlin.ru/appears/2008/11/26/2252_type63377type63380_209801.shtml*
3. BBC World Service Poll. February 6, 2009, *http://www.worldpublicopinion.org/pipa/pdf/feb09/BBCEvals_Feb09_rpt.pdf*
4. For more details, see Sergey, Lounev (2007). "Russia: From Europe to Asia or between Europe and Asia?" in *Russian Civilization*, edited by A. Patnaik, A. Mohanty, N.S. Kirabaev, M.M. Mchedlova. New Delhi: FK Publications; Sergey,

Lounev (2008). "Russia and Europe: The end of the honeymoon?" *Reinventing and Reinvigorating EU-Russia Relations*, edited by Clesse A. and A. Kortunov Amsterdam: Dutch University Press. pp. 209-227.

5. Ministry of Commerce and Industry. Department of Commerce. Export Import Bank Data, New Delhi: Government of India. *http://commerce.nic.in/eidb/iecnt.asphttp://commerce.nic.in/eidb/iecnt.asp*
6. The Ministry of Foreign Relations of the Russian Federation. Information and Press Department, "Asia-Pacific dimension of foreign policy of Russia". *http://www.ln.mid.ru/brp_4.nsf/itogi/0B60DA745F93EA81C325752E0036EB0C*
7. *International Energy Outlook 2003*. Paris, International Energy Agency, 2003.
8. *https://www.cia.gov/library/publications/the-world-factbook/geos/in.html*
9. *International Energy Outlook 2003*. Paris, International Energy Agency, 2003.
10. Mehdudia, Sujay (2008). "India keen to import LNG", *The Hindu*. November 8.
11. "Russian business net", *http://www.rb.ru/topstory/business/2008/02/11/133346.html*
12. "Russia seeks to diversify trade ties", *The Hindu*. March 08, 2008.

7 Indo-Russian Economic Linkages

A Critical Assessment

Gulshan Sachdeva

An important aspect of the old Indo-Soviet friendship was a special bilateral trade and economic relationship. Although this arrangement had many of the usual weaknesses like corruption, patronage, transactions in low quality products, it helped many small and medium sized private Indian companies to become exporters. After the disintegration of the Soviet Union, this relationship has been badly damaged. Economic transformation in Russia from a centrally planned economy to a market economy in 1992 coincided with the policies of economic liberalisation in India. These developments changed the nature and character of foreign economic relations in both the countries. Therefore, despite having solid economic and trade relations in the past, most Russian and Indian companies are still struggling to adjust in each other's markets. This chapter attempts to critically understand present realities of Indo-Russian trade and other economic relations. It is argued that economic changes in both the countries had adverse impact on bilateral economic ties. Economic relations are still surviving mainly because of defence purchases and some public sector investments by India. The "special relationship" is limited mainly to arms trade and defence technology. Private commercial initiatives are slow to take advantage from Russian economic transformation. Despite good intentions, both the governments have not been able to facilitate any major economic initiative which could have given a new direction to bilateral economic ties.

Background of Trading Linkages

Since 1953, when the first trade agreement took place, seven long-term agreements were signed between the two countries up to the collapse of the USSR. This bilateral trade was conducted through a specific system of trade and payment, called Rupee Trade System based on annual plans. The important aspect of the system was payments in non-convertible currency. The trade turnover between the two countries increased from less than Rs. 2 crore in 1953 to about Rs. 8,000 crore in 1990-91. In 1990-91, more than 16 per cent of Indian exports went to USSR and about 6 per cent imports came from it.

Table 7.1

India-USSR Trade Relations, 1960-61 to 1990-91

Year	*Exports (Rs. Crore)*	*% Share in Total Exports*	*Imports (Rs. Crore)*	*% Share in Total Imports*
1960-61	29	4.5	16	1.4
1970-71	210	13.7	106	6.5
1980-81	1226	18.3	1014	8.1
1990-91	5255	16.1	2528	5.9

Source: Economic Survey 2000-01, Ministry of Finance, Government of India.

One of the most striking characteristics of the Soviet's centrally planned economy was that it had created a system of exchange in non-convertible currencies with many of its trading partners. This trade behaviour existed not only with the Council for Mutual Economic Assistance (CMEA) member countries, but also with some other friendly countries like India. Similar to the "convertible Rouble", the value of exchange between the Rouble and Indian currency Rupee was arrived through periodic bureaucratic negotiations.

Most of the ideologically motivated scholars in India regarded this arrangement as the Soviet version of bilateral aid. The 'mainstream' academia in India also declared that India had "derived substantial benefits from its trade with the socialist world".[1] In the late seventies and early eighties, a few scholars in India had already warned that despite short-term gains, this type of arrangement would harm long-term requirements of efficiency and growth.[2] After initial industrialisation, India had problems of importing further machinery either for joint production for third countries or for the exclusive production for the Socialist bloc. India did not want Soviet participation in those areas where it could get markets of its own. It also did not want "captive units" whose production could not be exported anywhere else but to the Soviet bloc, and could provide the Soviets an opportunity to dictate terms.[3] Except for a few, scholars in India by and large did not bother to critically examine this production pattern, as the whole arrangement reflected political imperatives rather than economic rationality. This is evident from the views of a scholar who wrote that "the rupee-rouble rate is notional in the sense that it is an artificial rate of exchange between two inconvertible currencies. All kind of sophisticated arguments, theoretical or otherwise, are applied while negotiating the rate, and since both currencies have a notional relationship with the basket of western currencies, it is fact that the rate is equally unfavourable or favourable to both sides".[4] Some others, however, argued that even in a system of bilateral trade with a non-convertible medium of exchange, the exchange rate does affect trade performance, particularly when the trading partners are not both centrally planned economies.[5] After the Soviet break-up, the new policy elite in Russia also found these "irrational" arrangements with developing countries unaffordable. The haste with which bilateral payment arrangements were scrapped in favour of payments in convertible currencies indicate that Russian and Indian policy makers considered such bilateral arrangements undesirable under new economic policy regimes in both the countries.[6]

After the collapse of the Soviet Union, Indian and Russian governments renegotiated the entire trade regime. The 1993 agreement terminated the traditional Rupee trade arrangement and mandated all bilateral trade transactions to be conducted on hard currency basis. But with this agreement, the issue of repayment of civilian and military loans taken by India from the former USSR also came up. Finally, after prolonged negotiations, the Rouble credit was denominated in Rupees and a repayment schedule was drawn up. The agreement provided for an annual repayment of about US$ 1 billion equivalent in Rupees to Russia over a period of 12 years starting from 1994, with smaller amounts for a further period of 33 years. The Rupee debt funds were to be used by the Russian side for import of goods and trade related services from India. The Rupee debt funds are maintained in a central account with the Reserve Bank of India. Under a 3-year perspective plan, which came to an end in 1997, a part of the Rupee debt funds was allocated for import of tea, tobacco, soyameal and pharmaceuticals to designated Russian agencies. The balance was either auctioned or allocated to various states or importing organisations in Russia. In January 1998, this mechanism was replaced with a weekly auction of Rupee debt funds conducted by the Vnesheconombank (Bank for Foreign Economic Affairs). During 1999, allocations made for import of pharmaceuticals and medical equipment from India were utilised by several Ministries of the Russian Federation. Between 2000 and 2006, the utilisation of Rupee funds continued through auctions. In 2007, it was agreed that India's restructured Rupee debt will be invested in Russian projects in India.[7] According to Indian Finance Ministry sources, in December 2007, India owed US$1.97 billion debt to Russia under this category.[8]

Contemporary Trading Ties

As a result of these changes, contemporary trade between India and Russia is based on payments in freely convertible currencies. All Russian exports to India follow the new system. However, in the nineties, about two-third of Indian exports were financed through the renegotiated Rupee-debt repayment mechanism. As a result of all these economic policy changes, traditional actors in Indo-Russian trade and other economic relations like the public sector units and state trading corporations are no longer as relevant as they used to be in the Soviet era. Sections of the Indian private sector, which used to get away with selling many products of questionable quality under the bilateral system, also found it difficult to adjust to radically changed economic and commercial environment in Russia, driven by market forces.

Table 7.2

India-Russia Trade, 1993-94 to 2007-08 (in US$ million)

Year	*Exports*	*% Share of Total Indian Exports*	*Imports*	*% Share of Total Indian Imports*	*Total Trade*	*% Share of Total Indian Trade*
1993-94	648.60	2.92	256.89	1.10	905.49	1.98
1994-95	807.38	3.07	504.54	1.76	1311.92	2.39
1995-96	1046.55	3.29	857.53	2.33	1904.09	2.78
1996-97	811.84	2.42	628.96	1.61	1440.8	1.98
1997-98	954.12	2.72	679.02	1.63	1633.14	2.13
1998-99	706.26	2.14	545.42	1.29	1254.68	1.66
1999-2000	948.99	2.58	623.94	1.25	1572.93	1.82
2000-01	869.93	1.97	517.19	1.03	1387.12	1.47
2001-02	796.83	1.82	538.36	1.05	1332.19	1.41
2002-03	704.00	1.34	592.61	0.96	1296.61	1.14
2003-04	713.76	1.12	959.63	1.23	1673.39	1.18
2004-05	631.26	0.76	1322.74	1.19	1954.01	1.00
2005-06	733.15	0.71	2022.19	1.36	2755.33	1.09
2006-07	902.17	0.71	2407.61	1.30	3309.78	1.06
2007-08	939.74	0.58	2468.49	0.98	3408.23	0.82
2008-09 (Apr-Dec)	805.44				3773.32	

Source: Department of Commerce, Ministry of Commerce & Industry, Government of India.

Although Indo-Russian trade has improved in the last few years, it is less than one per cent of total Indian trade. This indicates that when it comes to commerce, both nations have moved very far from each other. These statistics, however, may not reveal the full story. Some imports from Russia, particularly metal, metal scrap, fertilisers, paper and paper products may be sourced through international suppliers. So they are not reflected in these figures. Similarly, many Indian goods enter Russia via "shuttle trade" or through third countries. Still, this will not significantly change the broader picture.

Table 7.3

A. Commodity Composition of Indo-Russian Trade

Commodity	*2006-07*	*2007-08*
Wheat	449.00	285.99
Sunflower seed oil crude	19.98	
Salt; sulphur; earths and stone; plastering materials, lime and cement	40.17	57.12
Mineral fuels, mineral oils and products of their distillation; bituminous substances; mineral waxes	176.18	153.19
Inorganic chemicals	31.35	35.15
Organic chemicals	55.10	142.35
Fertilisers	314.54	274.24
Plastic and articles thereof	5.36	5.79
Rubber and articles thereof	110.50	126.02
Paper and paperboard; articles of paper pulp, of paper or of paperboard	94.96	75.88
Printed books, newspapers, etc.	17.51	13.65
Natural or cultured pearls, precious or semi-precious stones etc.	53.66	97.18
Iron and steel	479.97	506.80
Articles of iron or steel	9.33	16.64
Copper and articles thereof	66.32	125.70
Nickel and articles thereof	192.71	255.24
Aluminum and articles thereof	4.41	3.81
Zinc and articles thereof	9.86	3.38
Other base metals; cermets; articles thereof	5.46	6.00
Nuclear reactors, boilers, machinery and mechanical appliances; parts thereof	67.07	96.17
Electrical machinery and equipment and parts thereof; sound recorders and reproducers, television image and sound recorders etc.	8.23	27.44
Aircraft, spacecraft and parts thereof	81.77	21.39
Ships, boats and floating structures	13.06	0.36
Optical, photographic cinematographic measuring, checking precision, medical or surgical instruments etc.	6.35	23.91
Project goods; some special uses	60.02	68.88
Total	2,407.61	2,469.70

B. Some Important Imports from Russia, 2006-07 and 2007-08 (US$ Million)

Commodity	*2006-07*	*2007-08*
Edible vegetables and certain roots and tubers	8.07	7.04
Edible fruit and nuts; peel or citrus fruit or melons	10.29	9.07
Tea	61.31	69.88
Coffee	6.71	5.72
Rice	13.36	5.96
Oil seeds and olea.; fruits; misc.; grains, seeds and fruit; industrial or medicinal plants	7.72	3.35
Lac; gums, resins and other vegetable saps and extracts	5.44	6.00
Preparations of vegetables, fruit, nuts or other parts of plants	25.27	17.83
Miscellaneous edible preparations	44.55	35.26
Unmanufactured tobacco and tobacco refuse	28.86	28.99
Organic chemicals	14.15	20.50
Pharmaceutical products	280.37	298.00
Tanning or dyeing extracts; pigments and other colouring matter; paints; putty; inks	13.48	15.48
Essential oils and resinoids; perfumery, cosmetic or toilet preparations	4.00	4.54
Miscellaneous chemical products	5.14	5.60
Plastic and articles thereof	24.76	18.87
Rubber and articles thereof	5.93	6.10
Raw hides and skins (other than fur skins) and leather	12.30	9.89
Paper and paperboard; articles of paper pulp, of paper or of paperboard	6.45	3.37
Printed books, newspapers, pictures and other products of the printing industry; manuscripts, typescripts and plans	1.09	0.53
Cotton	30.67	43.78
Articles of apparel and clothing accessories, knitted or crocheted	63.09	51.00
Articles of apparel and clothing accessories, not knitted or crocheted	6.88	9.04
Other made up textile articles; sets; warm clothing and warm textile articles; rags	3.88	3.31
Footwear, gaiters and the like; parts of such articles	3.81	4.68
Articles of stone, plaster, cement, asbestos, mica or similar materials	6.10	11.37
Iron and steel	32.17	26.47
Articles of iron or steel	5.88	12.79
Aluminum and articles thereof	3.41	2.46
Tools implements, cutlery, spoons and forks, of base metal; parts thereof of base metal	6.27	9.85
Nuclear reactors, boilers, machinery and mechanical appliances; parts thereof	36.45	50.11

Contd...

...contd...

Commodity	*2006-07*	*2007-08*
Electrical machinery and equipment and parts thereof; sound recorders and reproducers, television image and sound recorders and reproducers, and parts	40.72	14.26
Vehicles other than railway or tramway rolling stock, and parts and accessories thereof	5.27	7.60
Parts of goods of HDG no. 8801 and 8802	16.40	45.46
Optical, photographic cinematographic measuring, checking precision, medical or surgical inst.	7.98	4.03
Total	902.17	940.20

Source: Export Import Databank, Ministry of Commerce and Industry, Government of India.

The main items of traditional exports from India are pharmaceuticals, tea, coffee, readymade garments, cotton, tobacco, edible preparations, iron and steel etc. Recently, some non-traditional items like machinery have also shown some growth. Imports from Russia include iron and steel, fertiliser, wheat, minerals, chemicals, paper, rubber, copper, nickel, nuclear machinery, project goods, etc.

Apart from goods, services trade may become significant in coming years. According to the Russian Central Bank, India and Russia had about $680 million services trade in 2008.[9] Russian services exports are mainly associated with construction and maintenance of equipment. In the last two years, services trade has gone in favour of India. Indian exports in this category have increased from $90 million in 2003 to about $500 million in 2008.

Table 7.4

India-Russia Services Trade (thousands of US dollars)

Year	*Russian Exports to India*	*Russian Imports from India*	*Total Trade*
2003	442,875	90,130	535,005
2004	214,886	107,085	321,971
2005	192,291	96,154	288,445
2006	208,887	133,941	342,828
2007	235,575	217,619	453,134
2008	177,704	502,171	679,875

Source: The Central Bank of the Russian Federation.

State Linkages: Since 1992, more than a dozen summit level meetings have taken place and about 130 agreements have been signed between the two countries. To improve economic relationship, an Indo-Russian Inter Governmental Commission on Trade, Economic, Scientific, Technological and Cultural Cooperation has been working towards promoting bilateral cooperation. So far 14 sessions of the Commission have taken place. The Commission covers 11 joint working groups *viz.*, trade and economic cooperation; pharmaceutical; petroleum; coal industry; metallurgy; science & technology; cultural cooperation; information technology; power and energy; environment and natural resources and cooperation with the regions. Some infrastructural projects are being implemented with Russian participation. India and Russia have also cooperated in the oil and gas sector.

A major turning point in bilateral relationship was the signing of the "strategic partnership" between the two countries during the visit of Russian President Vladimir Putin to India in October 2000. Broadly this agreement meant enhanced cooperation in the political, economic, defence and cultural fields. The agreement talked of "deepening and diversifying cooperation in sectors such as metallurgy, fuel and energy, information technology, communications and transport, including merchant shipping and civil aviation". To promote bilateral trade, it also talked of "further development of cooperation in banking and finance, and improving credit and insurance facilities". There was also mention of simplifying rules and procedures for travel by entrepreneurs and businessmen of both countries. It was also agreed to jointly explore the possibilities of regional trading arrangements with third world countries. Since then, summit meetings are taking place almost every year, with many more agreements signed thereupon.

The crux of all these summit meetings has been common positions on major global issues like international terrorism and desire for a multipolar world and bilateral relations. These summits have been a very useful platform for formulating common positions and responses to emerging global political and economic issues. However, in pure commercial terms, very little has been achieved from the Indian point of view, despite long, nicely worded declarations.

Table 7.5

Number of Agreements between Russia and India, 2000-2008

Summit	*Number of Agreements Signed*
President Putin's India Visit 2000	17
PM Vajpayee's Russia Visit 2001	16
President Putin's India Visit 2002	6
PM Vajpayee's Russia Visit 2003	10
President Putin's India Visit 2004	11
PM Manmohan Singh's Russia Visit 2005	3
President Putin's India Visit January 2007	9
PM Manmohan Singh's Russia Visit November 2007	4
President Medvedev India Visit 2008	8

Source: Press reports and Russian and Indian government websites.

Although it can be argued that under new circumstances, business in both the countries is no more the business of the governments. Therefore, it is up to the private sector to take advantage of conditions created by these agreements. Despite this, these high level visits could have been used more effectively to promote Indian economic interests in Russia. Compared to India, Russians have done good business during these visits. They enjoy comparative advantage in the arms industry, and India has purchased arms worth billions of dollars during these visits. Eight annual summit meetings in the last eight years were good opportunities where some special bilateral economic relationships could have been created, even under entirely different circumstances. In 2006, a Joint Study Group was set up to work out a programme for enhancing the bilateral trade to US$10 billion by 2010 and to explore the possibilities of a Comprehensive Economic Cooperation Agreement (CECA) between the two countries. The group submitted its lacklustre report in July 2007.[10] Except for the recommendation of CECA, there was hardly any specific recommendation. Still, this Group suggested a Joint Task Force to monitor its recommendation. Subsequently, a Joint Task Force comprising the Indian Ministry of Commerce and Industry and the Russian Ministry of Economic Development was set up in February 2008.[11] So far, nothing concrete has come out from these exercises.

Military Industrial Complex and Investment Linkages

Despite economic policy changes in both the countries, the Indo-Russian economic relationship has been largely dominated by the defence/public sector. In recent years, there has been some movement in the private sector. Strong economic linkage is still in the military industrial complex (MIC). In 1991, 70 per cent of the army armaments, 80 per cent of air force armaments and 85 per cent of navy armaments were of Soviet origin. It is an established fact that India still relies heavily on Russia for its arms. During the Cold War years, the former USSR and India maintained very close defence ties. Even today, India is the second largest buyer of Russian arms after China. According to Stockholm International Peace Research Institute (SIPRI) Arms Transfers Database, between 1992 and 2008, India bought weapons worth US$16.2 billion (at 1990 constant prices) from Russia. This is about 70 per cent of total Indian arms imports and about 21 per cent of total Russian arms exports during this period.[12]

Major Indian investments in Russia include ONGC Videsh Ltd., acquiring a 20 per cent stake in the Sakhalin-I oil and gas project, ICICI bank's opening its subsidiary ICICI Bank Eurasia in Russia, TATA Motors launching a project to assemble its light-duty trucks at Russia's Urals Automobile and Motor Plant and assembling buses at Volzhanin and Samotlor plants. The SUN group has also invested in Russia's food and real estate industries. Similarly, pharmaceutical companies like Dr. Reddy's Laboratories Ltd. and Lupin Ltd. have investments in Russia. Berger Paints has also started its operations in Russia. The Carborundum Universal has purchased an 84 per cent share in Russia's Volzhsky Abrasive Plant in the Volgograd region. Companies which are exploring possibilities for investment in Russia include GAIL, Indian Oil, Coal India, Reliance and Tata Tea. The GMR Infrastructure has presented a tender for the reconstruction and maintenance of St. Petersburg's Pulkovo Airport. ONGC may increase its presence in the market through its purchase of Imperial Energy, which has presence in the Russian market.

Similarly, many Russian companies are active in the Indian market. Silovye Mashiny and Tekhnopromeksport are providing equipment and technical assistance for the construction of the Sipat thermal power plant in Chhattisgarh, Bihar and Uttar Pradesh. Two 1000 Mw nuclear power plants in Koodankulam are being constructed with the help of Russian Atomstroyexport. AFK Sistema owns 73 per cent share in the Indian telecom operator Shyam Telelink. It is constructing a pan-Indian transmitting network Shyam, which will be launched in 2009. Russian VTB bank has also started its operation in India. Sberbank also intends to enter the Indian market. Many other infrastructure companies which are already opearting in India are Transstroy and Tsentr Dorstroi (road construction), Elektrostal and Tyazhpromexport (metallurgical industry) and Stroytransgaz (gas pipeline). A joint venture between Russian truck maker Kamaz and India's Tatra Vectra Motors is nearing completion. The unit will produce Kamaz-6540 dump trucks of over 25 metric tonnes and Kamaz-5460 prime movers. Zarubezhneftegaz is doing exploration work along with GAIL in the Bay of Bengal. Last year, Russian GidroOGK and SUN Group launched a joint venture called RusSUNHydro. The newly formed company plans to participate in hydroelectric projects in India. At the January 2007 summit, a decision was made to establish the joint India-Russia titanium product facility. In February 2008, Russia's State Property Committee, the St. Petersburg-based engineering company Technochim Holding and India's Saraf Group set up a plant in Orissa. Russian share in the project is 55 per cent, which is expected to be financed through Indian outstanding debts to Russia. According to Indian Ministry of Commerce & Industry, the total foreign direct investment (FDI) from Russia during the period between April 2000 and August 2008 was about US$60 million which is 0.09 per cent of total FDI inflows to India during this period.

Conclusion

Future bilateral economic relations will depend on Russia's importance to India's developmental needs and vice versa. In the past, USSR played an important role in India's industrialisation process. It had a comparative advantage in sectors like steel, which was central to its needs. India has to assess now, where Russia has a comparative advantage. So far India is able to develop linkages in defence production, oil and gas sector and nuclear energy. Indian industry has already identified areas of mutual interest *viz.*, information technology, pharmaceuticals, telecommunications, financial services, hydrocarbons, energy and power, oil and gas, food processing, financial consultancy, management services, textiles and diamond processing. The problem areas are well known for years. These include lack of information, visa problems, logistic issues etc. Still very little attempt has been made to address these issues. There was a lot of hope that North-South trade corridor would be able to tackle some of the transportation problems. Due to low trade volumes, the trading community has not taken to this route. Strong political will in both the countries to improve bilateral economic relations could have been converted into real economic gains if some imaginative initiatives were taken, particularly when the Russian economy was booming between 2000 and 2007. With global economic slowdown, things have become more complicated now. The present Indo-Russian commercial relations are certainly not commensurate with the existing potential. In the last few years, India has signed bilateral trade deals with many partners and many are under negotiation. However, unless Russia joins the World Trade Organization (WTO), it is highly unlikely that India and Russia will be able to sign any bilateral trade and economic cooperation agreement. In the last 15 years, Indian and Russian economies have drifted away from each other. With changing foreign policy orientation in India, the importance of arms imports from Russia may also see a declining trend in the coming years. With no major breakthrough, Indian and Russian economic ties will continue to depend on arms trade, nuclear and energy industry linkages. Russian exports to India are likely to be from the extracting industries, and limited Indian exports will continue to be from low volume, high value and high profit sectors.

End Notes

1. Nayyar, Deepak (ed.) (1975). *Economic Relations between Socialist Countries and the Third World*. London: Macmillan. p.xi.
2. Jayashekar (1983). "India's trade with the Soviet bloc: Growing dependence and commodity inconvertibility", *Problems of Non-Alignment* 1(2): 115-140.
3. Valkenier, Elizabeth Kridl (1986). *The Soviet Union and the Third World: An Economic Bind*. New Delhi: Allied Publishers. p.142.
4. Kumar, Suresh (ed.) (1987). *Indo-CMEA Economic Relations*. New Delhi: Ashish Publishing House and Indian Council of Research on International Economic Relations. p.141.
5. Sen, Proneb (1990). "Rupee-Rouble exchange rate", *Economic and Political Weekly*. March 24.
6. Sen, Proneb (1999). "Hard goods and soft currencies: A note on bilateral payment arrangements", *Working Paper* No. 2. New Delhi: Planning Commission.
7. "Russia to start 'restructuring' Rupee-fund from April: Gref", 15 February 2007 *http://news.webindia123.com/news/ar_showdetails.asp?id=702150133&cat=&n_date=20070215*
8. "India, Russia to benefit from old economic pact", 1 April 2009 *http://www.livemint.com/2009/03/31224839/India-Russia-to-benefit-from.html*
9. *http://www.cbr.ru/eng/statistics/credit_statistics/print.asp?file=trade_2002-08_e.htm*
10. See Report of the India-Russia Joint Study Group at *http://commerce.nic.in/publications/Report_India_Russia_Joint_Study_Group_10_9_2007.pdf?id=15*
11. See *http://commerce.nic.in/WhatsNew/WhatsNew_detail.asp?id=15*
12. For details, see SIPRI Arms Transfer Database at *http://armstrade.sipri.org/*

Section III
India and Russia in the Contemporary World

8 Russia and India in a Multidimensional World

An Experiment with Five Indices

Ivan Timofeev

The contemporary world is extremely heterogeneous. Its building blocks—more than 190 sovereign states—possess unique features and characteristics. They play specific roles in the world, have different levels and stages of development, articulate particular national agendas and have various political systems and regimes. Such diversity represents a serious challenge for the students of international relations. What factors determine the international structure? What kinds of variables predominate in the explanation of a certain country's place in this structure i.e., what features are the most characteristic for a particular country as a unique polity?

These questions are a matter of special concern regarding the new leaders such as Brazil, Russia, India and China (BRIC). What makes them belong to the same "club", apart from such obvious characteristics as economic growth and regional leadership? Do these countries have the same typological features? Do they face the same challenges, and possess the resources to counteract them? This chapter will strive to highlight these questions with special emphasis on Russia and India—the two countries with bright prospects of mutual cooperation.

The key assumption implies that these questions should not be approached in terms of a single criterion as to the nature of the political regime, "hard" or "soft" power, etc. Rather they should be answered within a multidimensional context, taking into account the different spheres of a country's performance.

Another assumption is of a methodological kind. The chapter relies on quantitative rather than qualitative approach, justifying the main conclusions by hard statistical data processed by means of multi-dimensional statistical analysis. It is based on the results of the "Political Atlas of the Modern World"—the project of Moscow State Institute of International Relations (MGIMO) University and the Institute of Social Design and headed by Prof. Andrei Melville.[1]

The countries will be compared in terms of five indices of the "Political Atlas"—the index of external and internal threats, index of potential of international influence, quality of life index, stateness index and institutional basis of democracy index. The positions of India, Russia and other BRIC countries in the structure of world polities, as revealed by the method of principle components and cluster analysis, will be under a spotlight.

Methodology

The methodology of our research implies a number of consequent steps. On the first stage of "Political Atlas", we gathered a quantitative database composed of about 50 variables for 192 countries—the UN members, and relevant for 2005-06.[2] These variables reflect different dimensions of the countries' performance. We conceptualised these dimensions in terms of five major factors, which were supposed to determine the place and role of a particular polity in the world system. Among them are the ability of the country to respond to external and internal threats; capacity to influence international environment; ability to maintain the well-being of the population; efficiency of the state; and ability to sustain key democratic institutions.

On the second stage of our research, we aggregated our 50 parameters into five indices, each corresponding to a particular factor, mentioned above. Developing the indices appeared to be the key methodological problem. One of the most tempting ways was to normalise the variables into a scale and count their average values. Being quite simple, this way, however, neglected the real weights of the variables, while it was obvious that the contributions of the parameters to the indices' scores must be different. To avoid subjectivity and bias in favour of common sense and our background, we could not ascribe the weights of the parameters ourselves. Instead, we implemented discriminant analysis—a statistical method which allows counting variables' weights and therefore making the indices more reliable and representative. That was one of the key innovations of our research. Having index scores, we could rank the countries and obtain five ratings on the basis of the indices. The following indices and their ratings were obtained.

The index of external and internal threats shows whether a particular country is subjected to the challenges of domestic or international nature; it also demonstrates the overall magnitude of these threats. The index is composed of the following variables: threats of external aggression, terrorist threats, territorial disputes, separatist and/or anti-government activities, non-violent secessionist movements, attempts of military coups, water shortage, undernourishment and famine, HIV/AIDS epidemic, excessive migration, depopulation, undiversified exports, constant trade deficit, dependence on fuel imports, potential natural disasters.

The index of potential of international influence demonstrates the capacity of world polities to influence the international environment by means of "hard", "soft" and economic power. We should stress that it indicates a potential of influence, however, not the ability of the states to use this potential effectively. The index includes such variables as: share in the world GDP, share in world exports, contribution to the UN regular budget, voting power in the International Monetary Fund (IMF), membership in the Paris club of creditors, permanent membership in the UN Secretary Council, military spending, regular army personnel (manpower), possession of nuclear weapons, possession of fourth and fifth generation fighter aircrafts, military stationing abroad, share in the world population, Nobel prizes (at least 10).

Quality of life index partly intersects with the United Nations Development Programme (UNDP) Human Development Index (HDI), though we have taken into account some additional variables. Among them are life expectancy at birth, death rate (communicable diseases), death rate (injuries), infant mortality, GDP per capita, public health expenditure per capita, involvement ratio for primary, secondary and tertiary schools.

Index of stateness demonstrates the level and ability to sustain the country's sovereignty and integrity. The variables of the index are the following: duration of sovereign stateness, share of foreign aid in a country's gross national income (GNI), external debt, foreign military presence or deployment in a country, casualties of internal conflicts (if any), internal conflicts: area affected, internal conflicts: impact on regime stability, ratio of patent applications by residents and non-residents, national currency pegging regime, share of ethnic majority in a country's total population.

Index of institutional basis of democracy is composed of the variables which indicate the quality of key democratic institutions performance. These parameters are: competition for the executive, parliamentary competition, electoral inclusiveness, duration of uninterrupted minimal electoral tradition (since 1945), continuity of democratic tradition after World War I, absence or disruption of competition for the executive, violations of constitutional order, chief executive tenure for more than two terms in succession, influence of parliament on government formation, share of women in the lower house of parliament.

Having calculated the indices' scores and having made the country ratings, we revealed the correlations between indices. It appeared that most indices are significantly correlated with each other. Is this good or bad for our research goals?

On the one hand, this is a positive result. We could observe the interrelations between our key dimensions. Thus, for instance, we found that the stateness index is correlated with the index of external and internal threats—the higher the threats are, the lower the stateness is. The same is true for threats and institutional basis of democracy, threats and quality of life. These results contribute to the longstanding debate in political science about the factors of democratisation, state consistency, etc.

On the other hand, the correlation between the indices contradicts our initial aim to analyse countries in a multidimensional space. If a particular index is correlated with another one, then a particular dimension has a touch of another. Statistically speaking, we faced the problem of multicollinearity which was a serious obstacle to an adequate typology of countries.

To solve this problem, we applied/attempted the principle components analysis, which was the third stage of our research. This method allowed us to get orthogonal i.e., uncorrelated dimensions of countries' performance and to reveal the structures composed of the countries in these dimensions. Our five indices were taken as variables and were reduced into four principle components. The weights of indices in the components allowed us the opportunity to interpret these components.

The first component is a projection of national survival and its quality where the index of external and internal threats and quality of life index have the highest weights and appeared to be opposed to each other. This component explains the largest share of variance (55.4 per cent).

The second component is a projection of democratic state basis. The stateness index and the index of institutional basis of democracy have the highest weights and are opposed to each other. This component explains 26.4 per cent of variance.

The third one is a projection which we called the "human cost" of stateness. The stateness index and quality of life index have the highest weights and are opposed to each other. The component explains 11.2 per cent of variance.

Finally, the fourth one is the component of international influence maximisation. The index of potential of international influence has the highest weight and it has no anti-focus. This component explains only 7 per cent of variance. However, we will see that it is this projection, which explains the most significant and powerful polities in a contemporary world, including Russia and India.

The final stage of our analysis implied the clusterisation of countries on the basis of their coordinates in the orthogonal principle components. Clusters were calculated on the basis of Euclidean distance metrics. The procedure permits clustering within the range of 2 to 191 clusters. We used 10, 25 and 40 clusters scales. This method allowed us to make a typology of world polities and to reveal differences and similarities between them.

Now, let us see the positions of India, Russia and other BRIC states in the countries' ratings, principle components' space and clusters, mentioned above.

Russia and India in Countries' Ratings

The rating of external and internal threats represents a continuum, where the country with the highest threats has 10 points, while the country with the lowest threats has 0. Both Russia and India face relatively high level of threats. The Russian score equals 4.34 of 10 while the Indian one—5.99 of 10. Suffering a wide range of different threats, our countries are still not comparable with the "leaders" of the rating. Among them are Ethiopia (10 of 10), Myanmar (8.26 of 10), Iraq (7.98), Rwanda (7.57), Laos (6.64) and others.

India and Russia have a number of common threats such as terrorism, potential natural disasters, separatists' and anti-government activities, territorial disputes. At the same time, both countries have a number of peculiar threats. In the case of Russia these are, first of all, the depopulation and undiversified exports. In case of India, the threat of external aggression and dependence on fuel imports.

In comparison with Russia and India, China also faces relatively high threats. Its score equals 4.48. The threats are a bit more intensive than in Russia and less intensive than in India. Brazil faces far less challenges. Its score is 2.16 and can be classified as the country with relatively low external and internal threats; though Brazil is hardly comparable with the representatives at another pole of the rating—Canada (0), France (0.12), Germany (0.77), Italy (1.05) and others.

It is noteworthy that the level of threats is not correlated with the capabilities and power of a particular country. The US, for instance, has relatively low level of threats (3.06), but it is higher than in case of European leaders as well as Brazil. America is threatened by terrorism, potential natural disasters and a number of economic threats such as dependence on fuel imports and trade deficit. The example of Japan is also quite illustrative. Its index counts 4.03. Natural disasters and fuel dependence are among the most serious threats. Selected countries' rating is presented in Table 8.1.[3]

Table 8.1

External and Internal Threats Rating: Selected Countries

Country	*Classification*	*Index*	*Rank*
Ethiopia	Relatively High Threats	10	1
Philippines	Relatively High Threats	7.47	13
India	Relatively High Threats	5.99	44
Iran	Relatively High Threats	5.34	57
Peru	Relatively High Threats	5.03	61
China	Relatively High Threats	4.48	78
Russia	Relatively High Threats	4.34	81
Japan	Relatively Low Threats	4.03	87
Saudi Arabia	Relatively Low Threats	3.63	101
USA	Relatively Low Threats	3.06	118
South Africa	Relatively Low Threats	2.37	136
Brazil	Relatively Low Threats	2.16	144
Germany	Relatively Low Threats	0.77	181
Canada	Relatively Low Threats	0	192

The rating of potential of international influence is led by the United States which has the highest 10 point rate. It is much higher than in case of China which holds the second position in the rating with 3.93 points. Russia has 2.60 points while India—2.28, occupying the 7th and the 8th positions correspondingly. Among other leaders are Japan (3.25), Germany (3.24), France (2.81) and UK (2.65). The first 8 positions in the rating are mostly occupied by G-8 countries, though Italy (1.95) and Canada (1.50) are replaced by China and India. Brazil is on the 17th position with 1.01 points. Its score is higher than that of Pakistan (0.92), but lower than that of South Korea (1.02). Selected countries' rating is presented in Table 8.2.

Table 8.2

Potential of International Influence Rating: Selected Countries

Country	*Classification*	*Index*	*Rank*
USA	Relatively High Influence	10	1
China	Relatively High Influence	3.93	2
Japan	Relatively High Influence	3.25	3
Germany	Relatively High Influence	3.24	4
France	Relatively High Influence	2.81	5
UK	Relatively High Influence	2.65	6
Russia	Relatively High Influence	2.6	7
India	Relatively High Influence	2.28	8
Canada	Relatively High Influence	1.5	11
Brazil	Relatively High Influence	1.01	17
Mexico	Relatively Low Influence	0.8	23
South Africa	Relatively Low Influence	0.49	34
Algeria	Relatively Low Influence	0.43	39
Chile	Relatively Low Influence	0.28	56

The major sources of India's potential of influence are represented by its growing economy, rising military power (both in terms of manpower and military expenditures), increasing technological capabilities of the armed forces (including nuclear arms and advanced combat aviation). Besides, India is one of the world demographic leaders.

The Russian potential of influence is also determined by its military power (though incomparable with the one of the former USSR) and recovering economy. Russian power is bolstered by its permanent membership in the UN Security Council and military deployment abroad. However, unlike India, the capacity of Russia to influence the international environment is being undermined by massive/significant depopulation.

Looking through the quality of life rating, we will find both Russia and India in the group of countries with relatively low quality of life. The Russian score is 2.68 and the Indian one is 1.60. The leaders of the rating are Luxembourg (10), Ireland (6.88) and Norway (6.86), while outsiders are represented by Central African Republic (0), Afghanistan (0.18), Congo (0.27) and Zambia (0.29) among others. Selected countries' rating is presented in Table 8.3. Both Russia and India have lot to do to improve the living standards of the population, though their problem is nowhere as acute as that the countries of sub-Saharan Africa.

Table 8.3

Quality of Life Rating: Selected Countries

Country	*Classification*	*Index*	*Rank*
Luxembourg	Relatively High Quality	10	1
Belgium	Relatively High Quality	6.14	10
Germany	Relatively High Quality	5.55	22
Korea (South)	Relatively High Quality	4.66	33
Argentina	Relatively High Quality	3.58	46
Brazil	Relatively Low Quality	2.83	65
Russia	Relatively Low Quality	2.68	73
China	Relatively Low Quality	2.35	95
South Africa	Relatively Low Quality	2	111
India	Relatively Low Quality	1.6	125
Pakistan	Relatively Low Quality	1.25	143
Yemen	Relatively Low Quality	1.02	149
Senegal	Relatively Low Quality	0.83	161
Kenya	Relatively Low Quality	0.34	185

It should be mentioned that the quality of life issues are different in nature in Russia and in India. Russia still faces negative social consequences because of the 1990s crisis, and the collapse of the USSR. It has relatively short life expectancy and extremely high death rates, combined with poor health expenditures per capita. At the same time the percentage of its population enrolled into the educational system is high.

The Indian quality of life issues are mostly determined by its overpopulation. Being an advantage in terms of its potential of international influence, overpopulation seems to represent a serious challenge for the national living standards coefficients. Thus, the Indian GDP is one of the highest in Asia, however GDP per capita is not that high. Enrolment in the education system is the lowest among BRIC countries. Health expenditure per capita is also a matter of concern.

In comparison with Russia and India, China and Brazil also may be characterised as countries with relatively low quality of life. Chinese score (2.35) is a bit poorer than the Russian one, though it is higher than that of India. Brazil (2.83) is a bit higher in the rating in comparison with Russia.

Stateness index demonstrates that Russia and India are quite vulnerable in this regard. Our countries face internal conflicts which challenge their territorial integrity. Russia has 7.50 points of 10, while India—5.42 (though both countries have sufficient level of stateness). China and especially Brazil have higher coefficients—8.24 and 8.39 correspondingly. Such countries as USA (10), Japan (9.34), Switzerland (9.17) and Germany (8.93) are the leaders in the stateness rating. Chad (0), Kyrgyzstan (0.08), Afghanistan (0.72) and Timor-Leste (0.74) are among the outsiders. Selected countries' rating is presented in Table 8.4.

Table 8.4

Stateness Rating: Selected Countries

Country	*Classification*	*Index*	*Rank*
USA	Sufficient Stateness	10	1
France	Sufficient Stateness	8.55	7
Brazil	Sufficient Stateness	8.39	9
China	Sufficient Stateness	8.24	12
Russia	Sufficient Stateness	7.5	27
Saudi Arabia	Sufficient Stateness	6.99	41
India	Sufficient Stateness	5.42	81
Algeria	Insufficient Stateness	5.01	97
Kazakhstan	Insufficient Stateness	4.45	111
Ukraine	Insufficient Stateness	4.35	113
Kenya	Insufficient Stateness	4.18	119
Cameroon	Insufficient Stateness	3.16	143
Tajikistan	Insufficient Stateness	2.01	172
Chad	Insufficient Stateness	0	192

Finally, the index of institutional basis of democracy demonstrates sufficient differences among BRIC countries. India is one of the leaders in this rating. It has a very high score—7.35 of 10, showing even higher results than USA (7.3), France (7.25) and the UK (7.12). Indian result is determined by high level of political competition and uninterrupted electoral tradition.

The Russian score is 5.24. It is in the middle of the rating, apparently combining democratic institutions with the autocratic legacy. The lack of electoral tradition seriously downgrades the Russian position in the rating.

Brazil (6.25) has a higher score than Russia, though it is lower than that of India. The Chinese level, of institutional basis of democracy, is very poor. It equals only 0.69 of 10 points.

Switzerland (10), Canada (8.42), Netherlands (8.38) and Denmark (8.35) are the leaders of the rating, while Myanmar (0), Somalia (0.02), Turkmenistan (0.03), Eritrea (0.04) are the outsiders. Selected countries' rating is presented in Table 8.5.

Table 8.5

Institutional Basis of Democracy Rating: Selected Countries

Country	*Classification*	*Index*	*Rank*
Switzerland	Sufficient Institutional Basis	10	1
Belgium	Sufficient Institutional Basis	7.99	10
India	Sufficient Institutional Basis	7.35	16
USA	Sufficient Institutional Basis	7.3	18
Italy	Sufficient Institutional Basis	7.02	24
Korea (South)	Sufficient Institutional Basis	6.62	34
Brazil	Sufficient Institutional Basis	6.25	51
Russia	Sufficient Institutional Basis	5.24	93
Turkey	Sufficient Institutional Basis	5.13	99
Singapore	Insufficient Institutional Basis	3.43	136
Egypt	Insufficient Institutional Basis	2.21	150
Iran	Insufficient Institutional Basis	1.76	161
China	Insufficient Institutional Basis	0.69	178
Myanmar	Insufficient Institutional Basis	0	192

Principle Components and Clusters: The Implications for Russia and India

The method of principle components makes it possible to reveal the degree of each country's explanation by a particular component. The prevalence of a particular component in a country's explanation demonstrates special typological features of this polity and its special agenda. The percentage of selected countries' explanation by the principle components is presented in Table 8.6.

Table 8.6

Percentage of Countries' Explanation by the Principle Components: Selected Cases

Country/ Component	*1*	*2*	*3*	*4*
Australia	98.4	0.7	0.8	0.1
Ethiopia	95	2.8	0.5	1.7
Libya	0	94.7	1	4.3
Tuvalu	6	90.5	0.1	3.5
Colombia	1.6	3	81.8	13.6
Peru	1	0.1	81.3	17.6
USA	1.4	14.4	5.8	78.5
Russia	0	22.2	2.2	75.6
India	19	5.2	2.2	73
China	2	56.6	0	41.4
Germany	44.7	12.6	1.5	41.1

One of the most interesting results of the project was the fact that both Russia and India are to a very high extent explained by the fourth component i.e., by the projection of the international influence maximisation. Russia's percentage of explanation by this component equals 75.6 per cent while the Indian one is 73 per cent. These rates are the highest among the world polities, including the great powers. Only the United States has a comparable score (78.5 per cent). The Chinese score is 41.4 per cent, while the Brazilian one is only 13 per cent.

Of course this result does not mean that Russian and the Indian power are equal to the US, and higher than in the case of China. It means that the role of great power is the major typological feature of these countries, while the agenda of other components is not that acute for them. Let us illustrate this point, revealing the structures composed of world polities in the principle components' space.

The first component reflects the issues of national survival and its quality. The countries which are highly explained by this factor either have high quality of life and low level of threats or they have low quality of life and high level of threats. To have a high share of this component means to have a clear misbalance in favour of one of these two alternatives. For instance, Belgium and Haiti have 96 per cent of this component. Naturally this does not mean that these countries are the same. On the contrary, they are the extremes. However, this contrast is conceptualised by a certain dimension—national survival and its quality. This opposition is well illustrated in Figure 8.1, where the coordinates of the first component are represented on X-axis. We will find Belgium and Haiti on different parts of this axis.

Figure 8.1

Countries in the Space of Principle Components 1 and 2

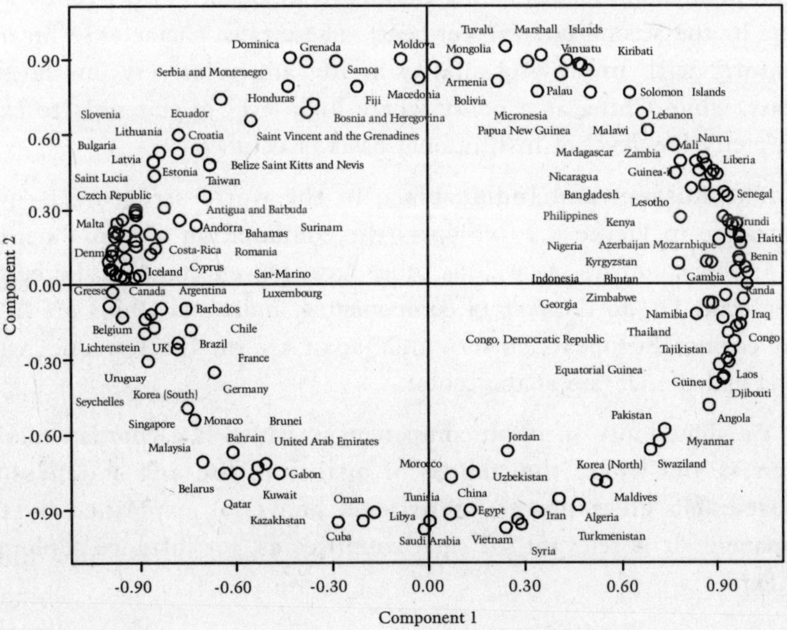

The second component is the projection of democratic state basis. Having a high score of this component means that a country is either misbalanced in favour of high stateness but weak in terms of institutional basis of democracy or, vice versa, has a high level of democracy though poor stateness. For instance, Vietnam and Tuvalu have 91 per cent of this component. Vietnam is an autocracy with strong stateness, while Tuvalu is a democracy, though having poor stateness, being entirely dependent on the foreign environment. This opposition is also illustrated in Figure 8.1 where the coordinates of the second component are represented on Y-axis.

Will we find Russia or India in Figure 8.1? No, because our countries are not explained by these components. They face serious external and internal threats and have much to do with the quality of life. However, these issues are not a matter of high extremity and are quite balanced with each other. The same is for stateness and democracy. Both countries seem not to sacrifice their stateness in favour of democracy and vice versa.

At the same time we will find Brazil and China in Figure 8.1. Brazil is to a high extent, explained by the first component (55 per cent), while China by the second one (57 per cent). These rates characterise Brazil as a country with improving quality of life and relatively low level of threats, while China as a polity where high level of stateness co-exists with pretty low level of institutional basis of democracy.

The Russian and Indian place in the world structure is quite illustrative in Figure 8.2, which is the combination of components 1 and 4. Our countries, as well as other great powers, tend to the bottom of the chart i.e., to the pole of component 4. India and China are in the right corner, European powers and Japan are on the left one, while Russia and the US are at the centre.

We should also mention component 3, which is a "human cost" of stateness and where the indices of quality of life and stateness are opposed. No great power, mentioned above, is explained by this component. It is relevant for such countries as, for instance, Colombia and Peru.

Figure 8.2

Countries in the Space of Principle Components 1 and 4

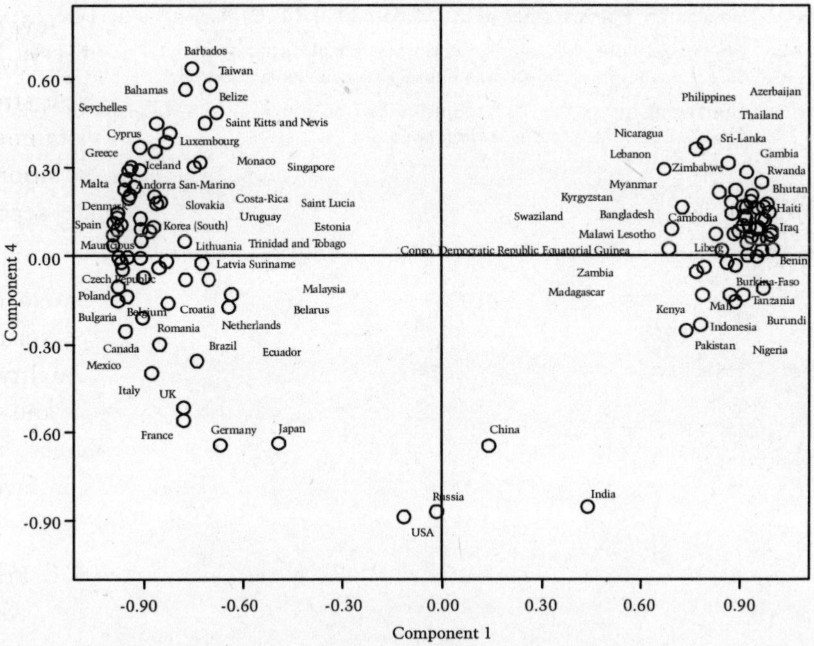

The coordinates of great powers, pictured in Figure 8.2, correspond to the results of cluster analysis. If we make a 25-cluster scale, we will find that a special cluster is made by UK, Germany, Italy, France and Japan. Another cluster is composed of USA, Russia and China. Brazil makes a special cluster with South Africa. India composes a cluster of itself—it is an extremely unique polity, combining high potential of international influence and developed institutions of democracy with relatively high level of external and internal threats and challenges to the quality of life.

The "Political Atlas of the Modern World" project is being continued. Our current goal is to make a shift from the "snapshot" i.e., the study of static picture of the world structure to the analysis of political dynamics of world polities. We strive to make time-series database and to implement new methodological tools to data processing. This new stage of the project must give new highlights of the specific paths and trajectories of Russia and India in the contemporary world.

End Notes

1. The project is designed by Andrei Melville, Michail Ilyin, Yuri Polunin, Michail Mironyuk, Elena Meleshkina and Ivan Timofeev. The English translation of the monograph "Political Atlas of the Modern World" is forthcoming in summer 2009.
2. We should note that usually world statistical data has about 2 years delay. The data, relevant for 2005-06 was entirely accessable in 2007-08.
3. The rating for all the 192 countries can be found on the webpage of "Political Atlas". See *http://www.worldpolities.org/*

9 The National Interests of Russia in the Asia Pacific Region

Dmitri V. Streltsov

The last decade changed the foreign policy priorities of Russia, which made an intensive shift towards the Asia Pacific region. While positioning itself as a bridge between the East and the West, Russia pursues the multivector foreign policy approach which means that the European and Asian directions supplement themselves mutually in the interests of the general strengthening of global international positions. This approach would allow for the orientation of the Russian economy, extended in space, towards parallel integrative interaction with both the European Union and East Asia. Along with that, the political and economic relationship with East Asian states cannot conflict with the European identity of Russia.

There exist several reasons for this strategic choice. First, Russia has adopted the principal concept of a multipolar world. Positioning itself as one of the poles, Russia must establish constructive relations with all potential poles of the world. Russia has enough grounds to become a leader of the post-Soviet territories. It relies on its territorial size, human and mineral resources, economic, scientific, technical, intellectual and military potential. In reality, all the political leaders of the post-Soviet states, while being independent in foreign policy, are doomed to consider the Russian factor in all their undertakings. Still, to ensure that the idea of a multipolar world becomes a reality, Russia needs strong partners who will also champion the cause of a multipolar world as one of their basic foreign policy objectives. And there are many such states on the world scene.

The second reason for the strategic choice is the peculiar geopolitical position of Russia. The vast territory of the Russian Federation can be geographically divided into northern, southern, western and eastern parts. In July 2002, the President of the Russian Federation V.V. Putin stated that "the foreign policy of Russia remains global not only by its military or economic potential, but also by the geographical specificity of the country. Russia is present equally in Europe, in Asia, in the North, and in the South. It is natural that we have our interests over there".[1] On the one hand, it is necessary for Russia to deepen its economic and political integration with the dynamically developing Asia Pacific Region. On the other hand, Russia needs to strengthen internal integration of the Russian regions, especially Eastern Siberia and the Far East, with the Ural Mountains and Central Russia, not to let the separatist tendencies expand in the economic development of the Eastern part of Russia. In other words, the strategy of the Russian Federation in the East must ensure social and economic development of the Asian part of Russia.

The multivector approach to its geopolitical interests assumes the formation and protection of national interests based on the geographical principle, given the regional specificity and the multidirectional character of the existing external threats to national security. The current state of affairs in the Asia Pacific region should be viewed as one of unstable equilibrium. There are several high intensity points in the region, including the Korean Peninsula, the Taiwan Strait, the South China Sea, Tibet, the Xinjiang Uyghur Autonomous Region and Central Asia. Each of these flashpoints has huge destructive potential and requires a great deal of care and scrutiny.

One of the main obstacles for the implementation of this strategic task is the traditional Eurocentric view of the Russian establishment, the lack of political will and the existing logistic orientation of Russia mostly towards Europe. The Soviet and Russian policy chronically suffered from an Eurocentric orientation and was focused mostly on western affairs. Due to old political and cultural traditions, Russia identified itself with Europe, so the European vector of Moscow's policy always dominated over the Asian one.

Formally, the social and economic development of the Eastern part of Russia remained a strategic priority for the relatively recent period of Russian history. Loud political statements on the "reorientation" of the Russian Federation to the East was periodically heard for the last 25 years, following the notorious Krasnoyarsk speech of Gorbachev in 1986. Yet, these declarations often caused a great amount of doubt, not to say disbelief, among the public. For Russians have a rich and, mainly, negative experience of then political masters making promises they do not have any intention of keeping.

The situation changed by the beginning of 2000, when the new Putin administration declared a new Eastern strategy. In 2003, the Russian government adopted the federal programme of development of the Far East and Baikal region until 2013. One of its central conceptual objectives was to stimulate balanced participation of Siberia and the Far East in the processes of regional economic integration in Asia. It was considered that economic relations with East Asian states would comprise an important addition to Russia's efforts over the development of the eastern regions of the country.

This concept, certainly, in many respects pre-determines the relations with the major economic partner countries on the Eastern frontiers of Russia. The total share of the Asian Pacific trade in the trade balance of Russia tends to steadily increase over the long-term. For example, it is possible to expect that in the following 10-15 years, the share in the Russian trade with six basic trading partners in East Asia (the People's Republic of China, Democratic People's Republic of Korea, Republic of Korea, Japan, Taiwan and Hong Kong) will account for 20 per cent of its gross foreign trade.

While considering the involvement of the Asian part of the Russian Federation in the regional economic relations of East Asia, Moscow aims to observe the balance between various partners and their specific interests which are characterised by a great deal of complexity. In such conditions, Russia cannot rely completely on only one partner, otherwise it risks entering into contradictions with other regional powers. Russia is consistently developing multivector cooperation with various nations not only on a bilateral level but also within the framework of key international and regional organisations.

There are several potential patterns of Russia's integration into East Asia discussed by academics and experts, such as energy and raw material supplier, transport corridor, donor of military or innovation technology, recreation zone etc. Some of them have already actualised, others are still under consideration. Of course, every separate pattern is an empirically formulated "ideal". In reality, the interaction of Russia with East Asia is much more complex in nature.

One of the more widely considered options is that of Russia as a raw material and energy supplier. The vision of Russia integrating into East Asia as a major exporter of timber, seafood, non-ferrous metals, fertilisers and other natural resources, has developed since the beginning of 1990s, the period of oligarchy capitalism.

In the 2000s, with rocketing oil and gas prices, this model changed its emphasis from "raw materials" to "energy resources". It was characterised by regaining state control over strategic oil and gas fields, the policy containing not only economic but also a political component. Unlike the previous decade, when massive export of resources was considered to enrich oligarchy, not to develop Siberia and the Far East, the realisation of this new model was assessed positively, with the view to its potential effect on social and economic spheres of the region that were suffering from severe depopulation.

Actually, this model accords with market tendencies, with Asia increasing its share of global energy consumption. The intensive economic development requires enormous quantities of energy resources. Today, Asia covers up to 45 per cent of the total global demand for oil. Besides, more than 60-70 per cent of its oil and gas is provided by imports, while Europe will reach such a level of dependence only in 2020. As East Asia is the fastest developing region, its dependence on crude oil imports will rise in the foreseeable future. This has prompted North-East and South-East Asian countries to display a growing interest in energy cooperation with Russia, recognising that Russia is the world's second largest oil exporter after Saudi Arabia, and has the biggest gas reserves.

Russia possesses one of the greatest world energy resources, with over 34 per cent of the world stocks of natural gas and about 13 per cent of oil, about 20 per cent of the reconnoitered stocks of coal and 32 per cent stocks of brown coal. At present, more than 90 per cent of Russian energy resources are delivered to the countries of Europe. However, in the long-term, more and more attention will be given to the countries of Asia and the Pacific region. According to the Russian Minister of Industry and Energy, Viktor Khristenko, the share of Asian countries in Russian export of oil will increase from today's 3 per cent up to 30 per cent in 2020 and natural gas from 5 per cent up to 25 per cent.[2] There are also important resources of non-ferrous metals such as boron, fluorite and tungsten concentrates, gold and diamonds, of which Russia's eastern regions are a major producer, as well as fisheries and forestry and a strong technology capacity.

In particular, Russia is an attractive destination for investment for Asian business. It is necessary to recall the successful realisation of the project Sakhalin-I carried out by large foreign companies from Russia, India, the USA and Japan. Actually Russia conducts the strategic infrastructural planning of its new centres of oil and gas production in Siberia and in the Far East in close collaboration with the perspective of economic development of the Asia Pacific region.

Russia plans to make its contribution to regional energy security by building pipelines from its oilfields to Nakhodka (Kozmino) with a branch line to Daqing in order to support the growing demand for oil in East Asia. The realisation of this project could considerably increase energy security in East Asia and will enable Russia to play a more significant role in regional integration; in these ways, Russia could support stability and economic growth in East Asia.

The strategic priority of Russia is the diversification and the multilateralisation of supply routes to Asian markets of hydrocarbons. In Moscow's view, energy supply formats should meet the interests of Russia as the producer of energy resources, as well as the interests of the energy consumers. Thus, the strategy of Russia is not aimed at knocking together, for instance, Japan and China, by giving any preferences to a particular partner. Moscow is interested in the development of clear and transparent rules on the energy markets of hydrocarbons, similar to those existing in Europe. Yet, staking on mere export of raw materials, without systematic efforts to stimulate the processing industry, will inevitably have negative consequences, turning Russia into a raw appendage of the Asian economy. Besides, the Russian Federation will never become a monopolist in the energy supply to the Asian markets.

Another widely discussed pattern of Russia's "soft landing" on the Asian integration system is based on the concept of so-called transcontinental "transport corridor", or the natural "bridge" between the markets of Europe and Asia. It assumes the use of the unique geopolitical position of Russia for the creation of transport corridors for ensuring logistic routes between Asia and Europe. It should provide transit not only by railway but also by automobile and air corridors, as well as information traffic.

It is considered that this model not only provides a global and regional market niche for Russia, but also promotes strengthening of interregional ties between European and Asian parts of Russia which is indispensable for the territorial integrity of the country. Besides, it will inevitably give a powerful impulse to regional investment cooperation, including the development of natural resources of Siberia and the Russian Far East.

With regard to the Asian part of Russia, this model was actualised in the middle of 1990s in the schemes of the Trans-Siberian land bridge, and the Eurasian land bridge (including the concept of Trans-Korean Railway). Besides, it is considered that the preparation of Asia Pacific Economic Cooperation (APEC) Summit in Vladivostok in 2012, would promote new forms of business cooperation with the business circles of China, South Korea, Taiwan and Japan in the field of railway and automobile infrastructure development of the Russian Far East. For example, the Japanese government has agreed recently to take part in the construction of the bridge from the mainland to Russky Island where the summit venue will be located.

Undoubtedly, from the long-term perspective, the realisation of this concept fulfils serious geoeconomical objectives. One of them is the low presence of Russia in the economic life of both East Asia and Europe, and its heavy dependence on external orders. Actually there is no powerful economic region in the territory of Russia, in the middle of corridors, that would independently generate powerful cargo streams both to the West and to the East.

As for other possible forms of Russia's economic integration into the East Asian growth centre, there also exist models based on the role of Russia as a developer of military and innovative technologies, or as a zone of recreation. These ideas are extremely attractive, and certain elements of them are being realised, but they do not have any distinct perspective now in the face of the declining scientific potential of the Russian Federation, its inability to commercialise the achievements of innovative development and the growing competition in the Asian markets.

It is appropriate to mention here several conceptual documents or statements by political leaders of Russia of the most recent period referring to the Asia Pacific vector of Russian foreign policy. From the perspective of North-East Asia, Russia's re-definition of national interests and foreign policy priorities have led to a new strategic engagement in the region with a strong emphasis on constructive participation and multilateral approaches.

On June 27, 2006, in his speech at a working meeting, President Putin made a clear formulation of the new priorities of the Russian Federation on the world scene. The Russian President stated the following: "Russia should bear the responsibility for the global social and economic development proportionally to its position and potentiality."[3] The president has directly referred to strengthening of the economic position of the country, and has suggested modifying the political influence of Russia in accordance with its economic potential.

Another important document is the Foreign Policy Concept of the Russian Federation announced by President Medvedev on July 12, 2008.[4] In the paper dealing with the priorities of the Russian Federation for addressing global problems, it is observed that Russia attaches great importance to establishing a self-regulating international system, an effort that requires collective leadership by the leading states, which should be representative in geographical and civilisational terms, and fully respect the central and coordinating role of the UN. For these ends, Russia will play a more active role in such formats as the Group of Eight, and its dialogue with its traditional partners, the *troika* (Russia, India and China) and the BRIC four (Brazil, Russia, India and China), as well as by more actively using other informal structures and venues for dialogue.

As for the regional priorities, the paper stresses the need for strengthening regional cooperation in the field of countering terrorism, ensuring security and maintaining dialogue between civilisations. Russia will continue to actively participate in the major integration mechanisms of the Asia Pacific Region, notably the Asia Pacific Economic Cooperation Forum, the mechanisms of partnership with the Association of Southeast Asian Nations (ASEAN), including the ASEAN Regional Forum.

Further strengthening of the Shanghai Cooperation Organisation (SCO), promoting its initiative for setting up a network of partner ties among all the associations in the Asia Pacific region, occupies a special place. The development of friendly relations with China and India forms an important track of Russia's foreign policy in Asia. Russia will build the Russian–Chinese strategic partnership in all fields on the basis of common fundamental approaches to key issues of world politics as a basic constituent part of regional and global stability. Bringing the scope and quality of economic interaction in line with the high-level political relations constitutes a major task in the field of bilateral ties.

While deepening strategic partnership with India, Russia will adhere to the principle aimed at strengthening interaction on topical international issues and comprehensive strengthening of mutually advantageous bilateral ties on all fronts, particularly in ensuring substantial growth in trade and the economic sphere.

Russia shares the interest displayed by China and India in building effective foreign policy and economic interaction in a trilateral format—Russia-India-China. It is of fundamental importance to Russia to bring about a peaceful and sustainable climate for Asia where there are still sources of tension and conflict and a growing risk of proliferation of weapons of mass destruction (WMD). Russia's efforts will be focused on ensuring its active participation in the search for a political solution to the nuclear problem of the Korean Peninsula, maintaining constructive relations with the Democratic People's Republic of Korea (DPRK) and the Republic of Korea, promoting dialogue between Seoul and Pyongyang and strengthening security in North-East Asia.

In his article in the lead-up to the APEC summit, held on November 22-23, 2008 in Peru, the President of Russian Federation Dmitry Medvedev presented his vision of the place and goals of this authoritative regional alliance and prospects of Russia's participation in it.[5] One of the priority topics of Russian foreign policy in the Asia Pacific region is the minimisation of the consequences of the global financial crisis and ensuring energy and food security.

President Medvedev especially stressed the topical issues as energy security, food shortage, climate change, trade security, as well as the issue of increasing social responsibility of the corporate sector as the most urgent items for substantive discussion and development of coordinated decisions at the APEC summit.

Serious attention should be given to the issues of energy security. As one of the largest oil and gas suppliers in the world, Russia will promote the creation of such a system of energy supply in the Asia Pacific region that would let consumers diversify the geography of imports, as well as ensure reliable and uninterrupted supplies. President Medvedev noted that Moscow is vitally interested in maintaining stable and predictable hydrocarbon prices based on the real ratio of demand and offer. Russia stands ready to take part in joint energy saving projects, and development of alternative energy sources as well.

Considering the problem of food shortage, the Russian President dwelled upon the unique agricultural potential of Russia which has been doing its utmost not only to fully meet its own needs, but also to help other countries. In the future, Russia seeks to become a major player in the world food market. Incidentally, in response to the food problem, which has been increasingly troubling consumers and producers, Russia has put forward an initiative to hold the World Grain Summit in St. Petersburg in June 2009.

Another noteworthy topic emphasised in the article by President Medvedev is the matter of security. In the first place, this concerns a joint stand against international terrorism which also seriously threatens trade and economic ties, as well as sea communications and energy transportation. APEC's work on the implementation of Russia's initiative on counter-terrorist protection of strategically important elements of the energy infrastructure is called to shore up the joint efforts aimed at carrying out these tasks.

Improvement of joint action in emergencies is another topical issue. It also includes the prevention and mitigation of consequences of natural and man-made disasters, and the fight against pandemic diseases. Mr. Medvedev stressed that Russia had accumulated considerable organisational and technological expertise in these fields which, as practice shows, has been used by the APEC countries. Only in recent years, prompt and effective assistance by Russian rescuers, who worked hand in hand with their colleagues, allowed the saving and protection of the lives of thousands of people.

President Medvedev is convinced that Russia's involvement in the integration processes in the region contributes to more efficient implementation of social and economic development programmes in Russia. And in this context, Moscow will attach great importance to strengthening industrial cooperation and collaboration in the field of advanced technologies and implementing transportation projects, including the establishment of a "land bridge" to move cargos between Asia Pacific and Europe.

The most important strategic goal of Russia's foreign policy in East Asia is to become involved in regional integration, primarily with neighbour countries and traditional allies, in order to have more opportunities to develop East Siberia and the Russian Far East. So the thrust of Russian foreign policy in the region support that goal. Russia hopes to advance cooperation with China, Japan, North and South Korea, and the ASEAN countries. Russia will try to maintain the balance of power and develop large scale economic cooperation with East and South-East Asian countries.

It is noteworthy to conclude on the following basic issues that could be formulated as long-term objectives of the strategic policy of Russia in the Asian Pacific region (APR):

- Russia must continue to pursue strategy of development of the Russian Far East, and its integration with the system of economic relations in APR;
- Russia should use the long-term interest displayed by Asian countries in creating an East Asian hydrocarbon market on the basis of Russian energy resources;
- Russia must continue participating in the multilateral economic and political formats in East Asia;
- Russia must promote regional cooperation with the US, Japan, China, India etc., while taking the initiative in those areas where the interests of all these nations coincide;
- Russia should strengthen military, political and economic cooperation with the republics of Central Asia;
- Russia should promote military-technical cooperation with the countries of the region, creating favourable conditions for promoting the trade of arms in the APR markets;
- Russia must develop cooperation with the USA in the sphere of military security in the APR, including the sphere of nuclear non-proliferation.

Russia shows a strong and long-term interest in all integration processes in East Asia, including the process of East Asian community construction. Its main motivation is to use the long-term interest displayed by other countries in its energy sector, to create an East Asian hydrocarbon market on the basis of Russian energy resources. Moscow hopes that the new integration model will serve as a locomotive for the entire East Asian economy, while the participation in its construction will facilitate the economic development of Siberia and Russian Far East. Russia strives for deepening national market-oriented and democratic transformations and large-scale cooperation in East Asia in collaboration with the US, Japan and China, while taking the initiative to find and use areas where the interests of all these nations coincide. In this context, it is important for Russia to develop permanent strategic dialogues with the US, Japan and China on East Asian issues, and thus prevent the formation of a tripartite American-Japanese-Chinese regional partnership without Russia.

End Notes

1. Speech by President of RF V.V. Putin during the conference with the Ambassadors to foreign countries, July 12, 2002.
2. *Epro,* No.2, 2005. *http://www.epr-magazine.ru/sobytia_fakty/faktura/dvustor_doroga*
3. *Rossiyskaya Gazeta*, June 28, 2006.
4. *http://www.ln.mid.ru*
5. *http://www.kremlin.ru/eng/speeches/2008/11/21*

10 India-Russia Strategic Cooperation

Eye on the Future

Nivedita Das Kundu

Russia and India today are different countries than what they were a decade ago. Both have regained their confidence and are aspiring to become global powers. The level of production and the size of gross national product, is growing in both the countries. Importantly, they welcome and acknowledge the achievements of each other, and understand the possibility of further strengthening the multifaceted relationship. They also appreciate the increased role that each country now plays in the international affairs. Both Russia and India aspire to promote a multilateral world order, even as they help strengthen the effectiveness of the multilateral mechanisms of cooperation with a central role assigned to the United Nations, and support to international law. The India-Russia relationship today is a major factor in international affairs, and their potential is far from being exhausted.

India-Russia ties though old, today there is a new emphasis to their relationship. Their cooperation is based on a constructive approach, which makes it possible for the two to work successfully on comprehensive expansion and strengthening of strategic partnership.[1] The analysis of this chapter is based on the hypothesis that India-Russia relations reflects the fact that there are obvious long-term interests between the two countries. An attempt has been made in this chapter to understand the current (existing) realities of India's relations with Russia, and future prospects. The chapter discusses the opportunities that exists between both the states in various sectors, and the challenges that they are facing in certain areas in order to continue their smooth relationship.

Military-Technical Cooperation

Russia is India's most important partner in defence cooperation. Their military ties occupy a special place in the entire spectrum of military technical cooperation. A major part of India's defence inventory is still of Russian origin and will continue to remain so in the near future. Russia is the only country with which India has a formal mechanism of an inter-governmental commission for military-technical cooperation, which meets annually under the chairmanship of the two defence ministers. India and Russia further extended the tenure of the Indo-Russian Inter-Governmental Commission on Military-Technical Cooperation (IRIGC-MTC) by another 10 years on the expiry of its present term in 2010.[2]

The basic implication of the Russia-India military-technical cooperation is that politico-military interests of the two countries complement each other, and that determines their mutual interest in further development of those ties. In addition, Russian-Indian ties are based on strong historic relations, as contacts between the two countries began back in the 1960s. It was Soviet supplies that ensured the development of the Indian armed forces, and it was Soviet weapons and hardware that India used in its conflict with its neighbouring states, including the victorious 1971 war.[3]

Joint participation in long-term R&D projects and joint production of sophisticated military equipment are the highlights of the current Indo-Russian military and technical cooperation. Military ties between the two countries are developing steadily and include joint R&D, production, marketing, regular cooperation between the different branches of armed forces, and joint training exercises.[4] In September 2005, the defence forces of the two countries held their first-ever joint airborne military exercise at the Mahajan Field Firing Range (MFFR) near Bikaner. The exercise, coordinated by 140 military personnel from both countries, introduced the concept of 'interoperability' against a counter-terrorism backdrop.[5] These kinds of exercises are being conducted on a regular basis both in India and Russia. One significant example of joint defence production is the BrahMos (Brahmaputra-Moskva) anti-ship cruise missile, which can be launched from submarine, ship, aircraft and land-based mobile autonomous launchers. Some 20 Indian and 10 Russian companies are involved in its production.[6] The project has a distinctly commercial angle, though the supply of the missile will be restricted to friendly developing countries. Now Russia and India are also jointly developing new BrahMos Cruise Missile i.e., BrahMos Block 2.

The two countries also signed an agreement for joint development of multi-role transport aircraft[7] to replace the ageing An-32 fleet of the Indian Air Force (IAF). Hindustan Aeronautics Limited (HAL) and Rosoboronexport will be the project partners. The investment of $600 million will be shared equally by the two countries; the Russian contribution will be paid out of the Rupee-Rouble debt India owes to Russia. (The envisaged requirement is 100 aircrafts for the Russian Air Force, 45 for the IAF, and sale of 60 aircrafts to third countries.) India and Russia have also agreed to jointly develop a fifth generation fighter aircraft[8] which will have supersonic manoeuvrability and cruising ability, long-range strike and high-endurance air defence capabilities. The development and certification of this aircraft is expected to be completed in the next six years. Indo-Russian defence cooperation also includes refitting of the Admiral Gorshkov aircraft carrier, which will join the Indian Navy, as INS Vikramaditya by December 2012.[9] However, some problems came up between the two countries when Russia demanded US $3.5 billion from India for the aircraft carrier, Gorshkov. This was the second time that Russia sought a price increase from the original contracted amount of $1.5 billion. Given the hike in its price, and the further delay in the date of delivery created controversy. Nonetheless, as the Gorshkov deal is symbolic of the defence cooperation between the two countries, this problem was resolved by the two states. India has paid an additional $102 million to Russia to speed up the Admiral Gorshkov aircraft carrier refit project. With the release of additional funds, India has now paid a total of $602 million for Admiral Gorshkov, which is currently undergoing repair and refit at SevMash shipyard in north Russia.[10]

The principal challenges that are affecting the prospects of Indo-Russian military-technical cooperation are a result of increasing competitive market conditions. The Indian market has always been open and competitive. In the 1960s and 1970s, the Soviet prevalence in the supply of weapons to the Indian armed forces was indisputable. The situation began to change in the 1980s, when France sold to India a significant number of aircrafts and Germany sold a batch of submarines. In the 1990s, Israel entered the Indian market and has by now become the second largest exporter of weapons and defence technologies to India, ready to crowd out Russia as the leader.[11]

However, India thought of diversification when the defence enterprises in the post-Soviet Russia changed from state to private and joint stock enterprises in an abrupt manner. This created severe problems for the Indian defence industry to adjust to these changes. Another problem cropped up when cooperation ties and production chains with former Soviet states were broken hastily. This created problems for India in acquiring spare parts for Russian made weapons, as around 22,000 different components were still being imported from various parts of the former Soviet Union (FSU).[12] Hence, severe problems were faced as many vital enterprises appeared to be behind the borders of Russia.[13] Therefore, after the disintegration of the Soviet Union, India deputed its defence personnel in the states of the former Soviet Union to find out about the defence factories or original equipment manufacturers (OEMs) located there, so as to establish direct contacts with them. But this approach was not appreciated by Russia; therefore, India had to deal with these states (for defence cooperation) through Russia.

Another problem that came up in post-Soviet Russia was due to the lack of transparency; crucial information mainly related to procurement and R&D, is still classified and details are available only to a few. It seems Russia's new commercial secrecy considerations persist; its traditional inclination is to restrict the availability of information. The data available in the public domain on defence issues is sometimes difficult to reconcile with data published in the various sources; most agencies are not even forthcoming about providing details. The decision process is, thus, becomes all the more difficult.[14]

One significant challenge that Russia faces in the Indian market today is that until recently, its offers looked ideal for the Indian market because of their cost efficiency. However, after almost 10 years of fast economic growth, and at the same time, with the demand for more high tech weapons growing significantly from the Indian side (the purchase of the super expensive systems as Poseidon is a case in point)[15], the situation has changed dramatically. Even so, Russia has till now maintained its solid position in the Indian defence sector.

One of the important sectors where weapons of Russian origin will continue to dominate is that of the main battle tanks. India has launched a major programme of direct purchasing and licence production of T-90s; it is now showing an interest in joining the Russian programme of the T-95 new generation main battle tank. Thus, it seems Russia will retain a considerable presence or even dominate, in such sectors of the market as surface vessels of the destroyer and frigate type, anti-ship missiles, air refuellers. Troop carrying helicopters might also enter strongly in the segment of aircraft carriers, and on the multi-purpose nuclear submarines.[16]

Russia's response to the new challenges that emerge in the Indian market, is a shift from simple trade relations between the seller and buyer to implementation of joint defence-industrial projects where the risk-sharing partnerships emerge. The creation of the PJ-10 anti-ship missile under the BrahMos programme became a pilot project of that kind. In addition, under the Multi-role Transport Airplane (MTA) project, the two countries plan to develop and produce, in series for their air forces, a medium size transport aircraft with carrying capacity of 18 metric tonnes. India is joining the Russian programme for creating the Sukhoi PAK FA fifth generation fighter, which has enormous political, commercial and industrial importance.[17] In general, Russia and India are still strong partners in the defence sector. For India, Russia is also considered as a reliable source of sub-strategic weapons like nuclear powered submarines or long range bombers. Thereby, along with the new challenges that Russia faces in the Indian market, new opportunities also opened up mainly due to the recent changes in the structure of the Russian defence industry, and its keenness to maintain its strong hold in this sector.

Trade and Economic Cooperation

The economies of both Russia and India are growing annually at around 8-9 per cent.[18] However, in spite of accelerated growth and immense opportunities available in each other's economy, Indo-Russian trade is still very low. Cooperation between the banking and financial institutions has picked up significantly in recent years.[19] However, proactive steps are required to boost trade, such as easing of visa regulations for Indian businessmen. The Indo-Russian shipment route also needs to be optimised. The North–South Corridor, the new route which connects Mumbai-Bandar Abbas-Astrakhan, provides the shortest route. The present route, which passes through the Suez Canal and enters the Russian port of St. Petersburg via Kotka (Finland) and Rotterdam (Netherlands), is long and time consuming but the proposed short route has not been commissioned yet. There is also the issue of utilising the remaining funds under the Rupee-Rouble debt agreement which needs to be settled.

Big prospects exist in the spheres of interregional cooperation and contacts between small and medium business. This is reflected in the developed partnership relations between the Russian Federation and states of India: in particular, between Astrakhan and Gujrat, Samara and Karnataka, Kazan and Hyderabad. Both the countries' business section are trying to interact with each other better, and know more about each other. Therefore, the establishment of representative office of Confederation of Indian Industry (CII) and the Russian-Indian business Council created by Trade and Industrial Chamber of Russia and Federation of Indian Chambers of Commerce and Industry (FICCI) is significant. Thus, Indo-Russian economic and trade engagement certainly needs a significant boost. The present economic engagements are mostly in the public sector. Of late, Russia has shown particular interest in cooperating in sectors like telecommunications, shipbuilding and high technology, including outer space.

Cooperation in the Energy Sector

Russia is expected to play a greater role in global energy security and at the same time, India's energy requirements are increasing rapidly. It is expected that by 2020, 45 per cent of the growth in demand for oil is anticipated from India.[20] Hence, there is need to improve pipeline connectivity between Russia and India. Some proposals are given by energy experts for possible pipeline connectivity between the two countries which both the countries are looking into, like the East Siberian Oil Pipeline that run from the Siberian city of Angarsk to China's Daqing, which could help India pick up Siberian oil from the pacific port of Nakhodka and would be a significant step towards creating a foundation for the Asian oil market. India's ONGC (Oil and Natural Gas Corporation-Overseas) has proposed an energy highway to construct a Russia-China-India (RCI) pipeline. The RCI is supposed to stretch from Russia through Turkmenistan, Uzbekistan, Kazakhstan, to Kashgar in China's Xinjiang. It could enter India via Ladakh, crossing the Siachen glaciers and the India-China Line of Control or alternatively through Himachal Pradesh, to supply gas to northern India.[21]

In the petrochemicals sector, Russia is interested in joint construction of oil and natural gas production and transportation facilities in India and in the surrounding regions.[22] India has geared up its energy diplomacy and is now moving quickly to penetrate the Russian energy market. India's ONGC Videsh Limited (OVL) and Russia's Rosneft are also jointly bidding for the Sakhalin-III project. Russia and India together could promote nuclear energy with the highest standards of safety and security in accordance with their respective nuclear policies and international obligations, as Russia is now actively involved in India's nuclear energy programme.[23] It is expected that in the near future, India-Russia energy cooperation will receive a considerable boost.

Other Areas of Cooperation

India-Russia space cooperation has also been growing significantly for the past few years. The two countries have agreed to jointly develop the Russian global navigation satellite system GLONASS to GLONASS-M and GLONASS-K. Russia intends to increase (with the participation of India) the grouping of GLONASS system to 18 satellites and a full orbital group of 24 satellites by the end of 2009. The two countries have agreed to jointly develop a youth satellite for educational purposes.[24] Russia has joined India's Chandrayaan-2 lunar project. India and Russia are exploring the possibility of developing equipment for earth probes.

Joint research in the area of electric engines for spacecraft and joint projects for probing the lunar surface and building a space based solar observatory to study X-ray radiation are also coming up between the two countries.

Among the top priorities on the Indo-Russian cooperation, are the traditionally warm and hearty people-to-people contacts and cooperation in the field of culture. By all evidence, the two nations are linked by in depth spiritual kinship, common features of national character as well as almost similar traditional perceptions of religion, literature and family values. Academic, scientific, educational, sports and other exchanges are being actively promoted under various sections of the culture exchange programmes (CEP) between the two countries. Of late, interest in Indian yoga is gaining fresh momentum. India celebrated 'Year of Russia', in 2008 and Russia celebrated 'Year of India,' in the year 2009. All these clearly indicate the growing interest in each other's culture and philosophy.

Conclusion

Both India and Russia assign considerable value for increasing bilateral cooperation. India too acknowledges Russia's resurgence. At present, the two economies display certain similarities. Both economies are resurging and at the same time diversifying. President Putin's era will indeed be noted as a transformational period for Russia as well as for the India-Russian strategic partnership, given that he was the major factor in revitalising the relationship after the Yeltsin years. He was also the architect of formulating strategic partnership between the two countries in the year 2000. Russia's present President Dmitry Medvedev also showed an inclination on further developing the Indo-Russian relationship. President Medvedev's first visit to India in December 2008, provided fresh impetus to the strategic partnership between the two countries. He made this visit to continue the tradition of annual bilateral summits established under his predecessor Vladimir Putin. According to President Medvedev, India is the key partner of Russia in the formation of a new world financial system and security architecture. He has also deep appreciation for India's socioeconomic achievements and balanced foreign policy.[25] This has reinforced the interests of both countries in maintaining close and friendly ties and in strengthening a multipolar world order.

Both India and Russia are developing fast, and therefore, there is a need to make greater efforts to strengthen forums like SCO, RIC and BRIC through which both the countries can maintain regional security, as well as enhance the cooperation in the sector of environment and disaster management, in pharmaceuticals, metallurgy, biotechnology as well as in tourism. Both India and Russia are aware of the fact that there is a convergence of ideas on various international issues. Hence, India-Russia strategic partnership will continue, and both India and Russia are set to take the ties to another level, keeping an eye on the future.

End Notes

1. Lavrov, Sergei (2007). "Russia and India: Mutually beneficial cooperation and strategic partnership", *International Affairs* 53(3): 24-29.
2. *Ria Novosti* (2008). "Russian, Indian defense ministers hold talks in New Delhi", 29th September.
3. Constantin, Makienko (2009). "Partners now", *Force* 6(9): 40-41, May.
4. *The Times of India* (2007). "India, China, Russia foreign ministers to hold talks in February", 29 January.
5. Flex, Yurlov (2007). "Russia and India: Partners in world politics", in Das and Nazarkin (eds.), *India and Russia Strategic Synergy Emerging*. Authors Press. pp. 61–74.
6. Unnithan, Sandeep (2005). "Cruise control", *India Today*, 2 May.
7. Dhar, M. (2007). "Indo-Russian relations are re-energising", *New Theme* VII(2): 26-27, April.
8. *Op cit*. Russia has also advanced a proposal for selling the advanced MiG-35 fighter jet to the IAF. (The agreement was signed on 19 October 2007 during Defence Minister A.K. Antony's visit to Russia.)
9. Prasad, K.V. (2009). "India, Russia close to fresh Gorshkov deal", *The Hindu*, June 5.
10. Ibid.
11. Ibid.
12. Cooper, Julian (2006). "Development in the Russian arms industry", *SIPRI Year Book*. pp. 435-436.
13. Russian arms industry still maintains extensive links with its counterparts in Belarus, Ukraine and with the countries of Central Asia and Caucasus. The Bishkek Dastan in Kyrgyzstan which produces torpedoes, is of particular importance to Russia. Moscow's Salyut aero-engine company acquired Topaz one of the best known arms-producing plants in Moldova. It also has interests in group of enterprises in Moldova and plans to form a holding company there. The Armenian

Company Orbit which produces night vision equipment was taken over by a Niznii Novgorod aviation industry firm part-owned by the Russian aircraft Corporation (Rossiiskaya Samolostroitel'naya Korporatsiya, RSK) for MiG. Kazakhstan has also declared an interest in integrating its 22 arms producing enterprises more closely with the Russian arms industry. There are also long-standing and close ties between Russian aviation industries in Uzbekistan, where Tashkent Chkalov works build Ilyushin military transport aircraft, in particular the Il-76, with 90 per cent of the components supplied by Russia.

14. Ruslan, Pukhov (2009). "A new dawn", *Force* 6(9): 48-49, May.
15. Ibid.
16. Sengupta, Prasun (2009). "Smash hit", *Force* 6(9): 44-45, May.
17. Trubnikov, Vyacheslav I. (2009). "Russia and India share a partnership of a genuinely strategic nature", *Force* 6(9): 37, May.
18. Gidadhubli, R.G. (2007). "India's economic relations with Russia: Performance and potentialities", in Das and Nazarkin (eds.), *India and Russia Strategic Synergy Emerging*. Authors Press. pp.43-45.
19. Mansingh, Lalit (2007). "India-Russia enduring ties", in Nirmala Joshi (eds.), *Evolution of Indo-Russian Relations*, also see *India and Russia: 60 Years of fruitful Relationship*. Delhi: Unity International. pp.28-37; January 2007.
20. Ibid.
21. "India's crude import bill surges 40 per cent", available at *Rediff News*, *http://www.rediff.com/money/2008/may/27oil.htm*
22. Tabata, Shinichiro (2006). *Dependent on Oil and Gas: Russia's Integration in to the World Economy*. Japan: Osamu Leda. pp. 1-7.
23. Information gathered by the author during the agreement signing ceremony of both Russian and Indian side during president Medvedev's visit and also signing of the agreement between Russian Rosatom head Sergei Vladimirovich Kyreanko and chairman of the Atomic Energy Commission of India Mr. Anil Kakodhar, on 5th December 2008 at Hyderabad House, New Delhi.
24. Pandit, Rajat (2007). "Russia to remain top arms supplier to India", *The Times of India*, New Delhi, January 22.
25. *Ria Novosti* (2008). "Medvedev identifies India, China among key partners", November 5.

Index

A

alignments, geopolitical 17, 72, 77
Antony, A.K. 25
Aryabhatta 39
Asia
  Asia Pacific Region 16, 20, 74, 99, 139, 140, 143, 146, 147
  Central Asia 79, 100, 104, 140, 149
    Central Asian Republics (CARs) 79
Atomic Energy Bill 85
Atomic Energy Committee 85
atomic power reactors using natural uranium 91

B

Baku-Tbilisi-Ceyhan (BTC) pipeline 79
Bay of Bengal 77, 118
Berger Paints 117
Bhabha, Homi 85
Bhaskara-1 39
Bhaskara-II 39
bilateral
  cooperation 115, 158
  linkages 83
  relations 16, 17, 21, 26, 77, 95, 97, 101, 104, 115
bilateral (*...contd...*)
  relations
    economic 19, 116, 118, 119
    political and trade 70, 72
  trade transactions 109
BP Statistics 2008 70
BrahMos (Brahmaputra-Moskva)
  anti-ship cruise missile 25, 32, 49, 57, 59, 61, 153
  BrahMos II 59
  BrahMos programme 155
breeder reactors using plutonium 91
BRIC (Brazil, Russia, India and China) 123, 124, 128, 131, 132, 146, 159

C

Carborundum Universal 117
Chandrayaan-1 45
Chandrayaan-2 45
China-India-Russia Strategic Triangle 79
Coal India 117
Cold War 27, 37, 40, 51, 117
  post-Cold War era 38, 42, 67
cooperation, regional 146, 149, 156

D

defence cooperation 16, 18, 25, 33, 34, 49-52, 57, 152-154
Defence Procurement Procedure (DPP) 54
Defence Research and Development Organisation (DRDO) 26
demand-supply
  complementarities 67
  synergies 71
democratisation 20, 126
Deora, Murli 100, 104
Department of Atomic Energy 76, 85
diamond processing 19, 119
disarmament 41, 46
Dmitriev, Mikhail 26
Dr. Reddy's Laboratories Ltd. 117

E

East Siberian Pacific Ocean pipeline 73, 74
Eastern strategy, new 141
Elektrostal 118
energy 13, 17, 67, 76-85, 98, 99, 104, 115, 117, 119, 142, 143
  consumption 98, 99, 142
    primary 99
  dimension of the India-Russia partnership 72, 80
  engagements 17
  global 45, 142, 157
  partner 70, 70, 71, 72, 73, 80, 81, 82, 83
  projects, joint 79, 83
  relations 17, 82
  sector concerns 72, 74
energy (...*contd*...)
  security 20, 45, 70, 73, 80, 83, 99, 101, 143, 147, 157
    collaborative approach 83
    India 70
  sources, diversification of 70
Enrichment and Reprocessing 90
EXIM Bank 77, 78

F

Federal Energy Agency 74
Federal Space Agency 45
financial
  consultancy 19, 119
  services 19, 119
food
  processing 19, 119
  shortage 147
foreign direct investment 118
fuel
  spent, right to reprocess 91
  supply
    agreement 86, 91
    assurance 91

G

Galileo system, European 43
Gas Authority of India Limited (GAIL) 77, 117, 118
Gazprom 77, 100, 104
geopolitical compulsions, larger 72
geopolitical concerns, larger 83
geopolitics 46, 95
Global Navigation Satellite System 18, 31, 42-44, 46, 51, 157
GMR Infrastructure 117

Group of Eight 146
GSAT-1 42
Gulf of Aden 52, 60, 80

H

Hindustan Aeronautics Limited (HAL) 31, 153
HIV/AIDS epidemic 125
Human Development Index (HDI) 125
hydrocarbons 19, 99, 119, 143

I

IAEA monitoring 90
Index of Institutional Basis of Democracy 124-127, 132
Index of Potential of International Influence 124, 125, 127
India/Indian/Indo
- arms market 32
- foreign policy 17, 49, 53, 77, 79, 97, 119, 159
- Canada agreement for the CIRUS project 86
- defence inventory 152
- energy
  - requirements 17, 20, 157
  - security 20
  - growing demand and dependency 70
- Hungary research and development cooperation agreements in August 1961 86
- import dependency 68
- industrialisation process 19, 118

India/Indian/Indo (...*contd*...)
- Integrated Energy Policy 68
- nuclear cooperation
  - France in November 1982 86
  - US in March 1956 86
  - USSR in October 1961 86
  - USSR in September 1976 86
- Russia 39, 42, 46, 49, 50, 52, 54, 55, 61, 67, 71, 75, 77, 80, 86, 89, 91, 95, 102, 103, 110, 114, 115, 119, 128, 152, 153, 158, 159
  - civil nuclear cooperation 85, 87, 89
  - collaboration 46
  - commercial relations 119
  - cooperation 17, 38, 49, 104, 158
    - defence 18, 33, 34, 49, 50, 153
    - space arena 38
  - defence
    - relations 35, 52, 57
    - ties 25, 26
  - military cooperation 34, 62
  - nuclear cooperation agreement in 1988 86
  - partnership 67, 72
  - relations 13, 15-17, 25, 41, 49, 53, 54, 158
  - space
    - cooperation 37, 38, 42, 46
    - ties 38
      - bilateral 26
  - trade 107, 110, 111, 112, 151, 156

Russia/Russian (*...contd...*)
geopolitical position of 140, 144
imports of natural gas from 72
Indian military-technical cooperation 152
industrial development 103
potential of influence 130
Russian VTB bank 118
RusSUNHydro 118

S

Sakhalin-I 76, 81, 104, 117, 143
Sakhalin-II 81
Sakhalin-III 76, 100, 157
Sasi, Anil 76
satellite navigation 43, 44
Satish Dhawan Space Centre 44
sea lane of communication (SLOC) 81
secure routes 72, 80, 83
services trade 114
Shanghai Cooperation Organisation (SCO) 59, 79, 146
Sharma, Rakesh 39
Singh, Manmohan 101, 116
Sir Dorabji Tata Trust 85
sovereign stateness 126
Soviet Kosmos-3M rocket 39
Soviet Union, disintegration of the 15, 19, 21, 39, 67, 107, 154
space
market, global 18, 46
sector 17
technologies 37, 38, 40
Sputnik 37
stakes, building mutually beneficial 82
Star Wars 37
stateness, human cost of 127, 136
stateness index 124, 126, 127, 132
stateness rating 132
Stockholm International Peace Research Institute 76, 117
SUN group 104, 117, 118
swap arrangements 81, 83

T

Tarapur Atomic Power Station (TAPS) 87, 88, 89
Tata Institute of Fundamental Research (TIFR) 45
TATA Motors 117
Tata Tea 117
technologies, state-of-the-art 32, 33
technology, transfer reprocessing 91
technology transfer 40, 41, 42, 53, 55, 90, 91
telecommunications 19, 103, 119, 156
territorial integrity 21, 132, 144
terrorism 18, 21, 51, 58, 79, 96, 115, 128, 146, 148, 153
textiles 19, 119
theatre missile defence (TMD) 78
thorium-uranium-233 cycle, research 91
totalitarian system 37

trade
- barter 27
- regime 109
- relations 18, 19, 70, 72, 77, 98, 104, 108, 156

transport corridor 18, 81, 98, 142, 144
transportation routes, cost-effective 83
Troika 20, 146

U

unipolar world 95
United Kingdom Atomic Energy Authority (UKAEA) 85
uranium
- atomic power reactors using natural 91
- low enriched uranium (LEU) 76

US Global Positioning System 31, 43
USSR/Russia nuclear supply rules 88

V

Vajpayee, Atal Bihari 38, 116
Volzhsky Abrasive Plant 117

W

West Asia 17, 70, 81
Western risk rating agencies 82
World Bank's 'Doing Business' rankings 82
World Nuclear Association 71
world order, multilateral 151
world structure 136, 137
World Trade Organization (WTO) 119